JOCELYNE SIBUET

with Catherine Deydier • Photography by Guillaume de Laubier

A FRENCH COUNTRY HOME

STYLE AND ENTERTAINING

Flammarion

CONTENTS

PRECEDING PAGES AND LEFT:
The magical charm of a holiday home is made up of a host of tiny details. Soft gray tones in Provence; bright sunny colors on the shores of the Mediterranean.

INTRODUCTION
FAMILY HOUSE OR HOLIDAY HOME:
THE QUINTESSENCE OF A LIFESTYLE

Deep in your heart, there is perhaps one house that counts above all the others. Like a secret garden, it conjures up memories, is nourished by intimate pleasures and by unique, special smells, by games played and by thoughts of a time without cares. The holidays. The house evokes tender sepia images of escape and indolence....

A place for a vacation cannot be just anywhere. It needs to be a haven from the daily grind. One may only be passing through, but this is where one regains one's strength, one can relax and live life to the fullest, without wasting time. It is a place where the present can be forgotten. Life needs to be lived differently there. Sometimes, indeed often, it is a source of memories, friendships, love. A color is chosen, and a whole state of being is created. Tiny things, intangible yet personal, summon up an atmosphere, an environment. For we all recall pushing open an attic door with a thrill of impatience, dreaming of mysterious, long-forgotten treasures hidden from all. Trunks teeming with photographs, fancy costumes, diaries, objects of all sorts....

A vacation home occupies, even if the visiting family doesn't own it, a special place in the lives of all who enter it. One of a kind, it serves as a hideaway, yet it provides the backdrop for new experiences, new emotions, which will remain forever etched in the mind, sensations that will never be completely lost with the passing of time. Its allotted task is to provide a roof for the secret life of childhood, sheltering an ephemeral world as comfortable to live in as one's home port.

Jocelyne Sibuet (above) never lets anyone else pick the flowers for her seasonal bouquets, carefully choosing colors to harmonize with the tones of the decor. Tartan makes for a calming atmosphere in a bedroom (facing page).

How can one fail to be moved by a once-resplendent interior slowly fading with each passing year? One has to understand and feel this deeply to be able to decorate such a house, to distill within it the reassuring impression of "déjà-vu," and make it worthy of receiving guests. In short, to design a suitable decor. And it is here that an exceptional talent like that of Jocelyne Sibuet comes in. Better than anybody, she knows how to create from scratch—or almost—homes in which people feel at ease, which they make their own, just as if they were actually at home and had always lived there. Or as if it cradled their past, their memories. It is like unpacking your suitcases in a house you have always known existed somewhere, like encountering a long-lost relation. Jocelyne Sibuet knows how to give people a sense that a place in which they might spend no more than a single day (or a week or a month), has always been waiting for them, and solely for them. This means they have to find their feet quickly, to get a feel for the place fast.

Through decor and color, and a host of other details, Jocelyne Sibuet tells stories taken as if from a family album, a life in which shared pleasures predominate. "We used to look for just this kind of hotel when our children were little. At the time we wanted special, beautiful, and individual places, offering impeccable service, that paid attention to the tiniest detail, but, above all, an environment that remained familial and convivial." After that, it is all simply a question of interpretation. And thus the Sibuet saga began.

In the mountains, Jocelyne and Jean-Louis run hotels that are elegant yet solid in style; in the countryside, they returned to the simplicity of a typical Provence country house. While on the shores of the Mediterranean, they came up with their very own version of the Italian villa. The modernity of the *bastide* (small country house) redefined Provence, just as that of Villa Marie reorchestrated the Riviera, and, in their time, Les Fermes—the houses built in Megève—shook up the stereotypes of the "mountain chalet."

"All these houses correspond to atmospheres I have dreamt of as ideals," the mistress of the house concedes. And, in such an ideal world, there can be no dreams without passion, without love at first sight. The cardinal rule in looking for somewhere to spend the holidays is to look before you leap. The attraction, though, has to be immediate. There's little point in conning oneself into choosing just any-old-place There must

emanate from the house something that finds an echo in one's heart, that individual, intimate touch. The Sibuets have always followed this precept when it comes to taking decisions. Coming into a given location, one's vision of how it should look and the story one wants it to tell, should be absolutely clear.

Both construction and decoration require meaning. The script is built up by exploring, gathering clues, following up ideas. Before taking over a space, one has to circle around it, walk through it, lose oneself in it, commit its configurations to memory. One has to leave it and return to it later. One needs to discover what links it to nature, its coherence, its presence; one has to draw from the surrounding landscape pictures to fire one's imagination and give life to the idea of the place as it takes shape. And then one must gather ideas, colors, moods, details. And such discoveries can take time. But that can be made up in due course. For, long ago, the ancients maintained a more intelligent relationship with the land they settled. They knew it intimately. They employed traditional building materials from the locality so that their houses melted into the landscape.

"We have always looked for places where one lives in close proximity to nature, without losing sight of our roots and of a certain spontaneity we are committed to preserving." So, be it in the mountains, by the sea, or in the country, in her Alpine fiefdom at Megève, on the shores of the Mediterranean, or in her Provence *bastide* among the vineyards, Jocelyne Sibuet thinks of her decors in harmony with the environment so they can adapt readily to the natural world. With astonishing acumen, she makes the space her own, breathing new life into it, yet without losing a sense of its continuity with tradition. Whether she makes them with her own hands, or leaves them "as they come," she highlights every element with little touches, details, shades, or harmonies, so as to respect the soul of the walls she appropriates. "Once a place has made its impact, the next question is to know how it can best be lived in, how one can make the most of it and reconcile past and present in it." But above all she achieves her effects by using natural materials, by taking account of local practices, and by breaking out of preexisting models. In the end, their sole objective is to create an atmosphere that is authentic— be it Baroque, modern, or functionalist—but without fetters.

Thus she and Jean-Louis have never been against mixing periods and origins. No piece is confined to a precise

function. They invariably prefer unpretentious furniture, useful, everyday objects which, in their simplicity, do as much to set the tone as the painted floor tiles, walls, and cupboards. This homely comfort is associated with smells, such as an open fire in the mountains and the aromatic plants drying in the country kitchen. Moreover, since it evolves over time, this cozy feeling gains from every successive association. Such diversity, though, can be given inner cohesion. "I like to imagine our guests take inspiration from us whenever they set up home for themselves," Jocelyne Sibuet confesses.

To afford others such pleasure, she has had to dream long and hard about the kinds of places that make a holiday really enjoyable. The mountains, the country, the seaside....

The Alps, Provence, the Mediterranean.... Whatever the region, building type, or style of these vacation residences, one immediately feels relaxed and entirely free in them. With the Fermes de Marie, then the Bastide, and the Villa Marie, the Sibuets laid the foundations of a tourism rooted in traditional ways of life, ushering in a wholly new concept—the "hotel village"—which took its cue from "cocooning", local charm, and the spa, at a time when such ideas were not yet trendy and when it was far from common to find double drapes in hotel rooms. These were what the high priestess of the trend in the United States, Faith Popcorn, today calls "hometels," a portmanteau word from house-motel-hotel. A new subcategory of luxury hotels like the W chain that make, she writes,

The simplicity and warmth of wood ensure a cozy, easy-going ambiance in the bedroom under the eaves. The head of the bed is inspired by the type one used to see in mountain farms.

"an effort to literally bring you all the comforts of home, including a rubber ducky in your bathroom, plus down comforters and VCRs/DVD players in your bedroom. It's an attempt to take the stress and strain out of traveling. The redefinition of luxury as a savvy recreation of the familiar is an example of the blurring that is permeating our culture: here travel blurs with life at home, just as the work environment is attempting to simulate those same comforts."

But make no mistake, by restoring a place to its authenticity, in bringing it back from the dead, Jocelyne Sibuet's prime concern is to make us share in the stories behind the location, and in its traditions. And the secret of her success lies in a natural gift for giving each project a soul. She respects what she has inherited, and, while anchoring herself firmly in her own period, relies greatly on the staunch values inculcated in her by her Savoyard upbringing.

In all humility, and in places that have a life of their own and which demand to be lived in differently, she tells us what the stones would otherwise hide from us. Like no one else, she can hear and interpret the almost imperceptible melody of every place she has worked in, adapting herself to it, communicating it through interiors that have proved a delight to every generation. Her "sets" are ones in which parents, children, adults, and youngsters alike can find their own little spot, their own niche.

"How we advance depends on feeling, on impulse. Before being entrepreneurs, we are creatives." And, for fifteen years now, everything has unfolded without a hitch: the right tone and harmony, content and form—and with a passion. Her greatest asset? Knowing how to adapt and rewrite the story as the fancy takes her—not only her own, but that of others too.

The Sibuets began their career revamping a dilapidated hotel in Megève, Le Coin du Feu. Working away at the oven and at the mill at an age when others were partying until they dropped, they were committed to reviving the comforts of the *hôtel de charme*, where guests should feel totally at home. Thus the first stone of the future Compagnie des Hôtels de Montagne was laid.

Today the company possesses three hundred hotel rooms in nine different locations. Self-taught, Jocelyne takes a hand in everything, from decoration to catering, personnel to customer relations. She had to learn how to do things and to convey her ideas. Passionate about mountain life (the manner in which she incorporates it into the domestic setting is wholly original), as soon as she could get away, she was off shopping around for things from the region, soon amassing a vast collection of vernacular furniture. She has thus recycled more than two thousand pieces of furniture, which have been restored, converted, or rehabilitated, often with little regard for their original function. Thus, kneading troughs become trunks, doors become ceilings, and dressers, walls…. No dearth of imagination here.

Meanwhile, the concept of the "hotel village" was taking shape, and the owner of the last greenfield site in Megève sold off his land. Jean-Louis worked on the foundations and spaces. From floor to ceiling, there were not only country crafts to be relearned, but newfangled techniques to master. He had a battle royal with these recalcitrant surfaces; contrariwise, Jocelyne had to overcome her chosen materials' lack of structure. He tore down, removed, rebuilt. She covered, coordinated, and added warmth. The mission, then as now, is to achieve that happy medium that puts people at their ease without their even wondering how. It comes from a way of organizing things, a subtle kind of expertise that relies not on fireworks, but whose end result is unadulterated comfort. It is an approach that trusts in time, too, in the same way that one lives in a house year-in, year-out. So it is just like home.

The Fermes de Marie opened their portals in 1989. The hotel was set in a small hamlet of nine Haute Savoy farmsteads built in well-seasoned Alpine timber. Each one was taken apart and every piece of wood numbered and reerected on concrete frames.

The image of this site has become a symbol, an emblem of the Compagnie des Hôtels de Montagne. More than just a sign and a company, it is a label that reflects a charter of quality, a whole ethic.

So that her customers can appreciate this marvelous yet family style of vacationing, Jocelyne has had to develop

The bed linen is stored in large baskets. Linen brings a note of color to this Provence bedroom, while the sobriety of the eighteenth-century armoire is enlivened by its positioning next to the Baroque-style, gilded-wood, side chairs. In front of the window, a small table allows one to write or read while gazing out over the garden.

From the decor of a bedroom, cozy in every nook and cranny, to the more convivial world of the table, where good eating is the order of the day. From balancing the flavors in a menu to the organization of a movable country feast high in the mountains. Fabrics, crockery, paintings, colors, prints: nothing entering the house escapes her. Her eagle eye extends to the vegetables growing in the kitchen garden, to the herbs and medicinal plants, and to the local farm produce she introduces to us with such enthusiasm.

For Jocelyne Sibuet is someone who likes to share things with her guests as well as to astonish them. Unlike the architect, every day she sees all kinds of people living in and moving through interiors she has dreamt up, but over which she relinquishes control. If she had to forfeit her "sense of property" long ago, she has fortunately kept her feeling for hospitality, a generosity she seems to have been instilled with from birth.

Today, what's more, she has returned to two early loves, and is redoing both the mountain spa and the beauty farm. Guided by the five elements—glacial rock, wood, running water, fire, and earth—she is also putting the finishing touches to her mountain flora beauty-care line. It is a holistic philosophy, and part and parcel of the same search for plenitude, for escape, and for harmony that motivated her when designing the hotels. It is another experience on what is a truly individual path—one that readily takes the mountain route, one devoted to the well-being of others.

So, the Alps, Provence, the Mediterranean.... Following in Jocelyne Sibuet's wake, this book throws open the doors to all her houses, peeking into the bedrooms, kitchens, and living rooms, venturing onto the terraces and out into the gardens. This is a personal journey orchestrated by an eye and a talent that are at once authentically original and utterly self-possessed. On page after page, this interior designer par excellence shares with us her ideas, her likes and dislikes, and reveals the details, the accessories that make the difference. She even lets us into the secret with a range of recipes, favorite delicacies, and local suppliers. It is an open invitation to turn the pages and experience for ourselves the tastes and pleasures of a vacation home.

an acute sense of spatial distribution. With years of experience, she has become a master in the art of creating worlds, and of presenting them in the most natural, unobtrusive way, as if this were the most obvious thing in the world. And it is second nature to a colorist who, with a few dots of color, can bring a room to life.

She scours junk shops and antique dealers the world over, in search of rare items or furniture that has aged nobly, as it might do in the attic of an old family home. She personalizes the interior of each house to accord with the season, combining all the ingredients that give life its savor; her guests come away with a strong sense of comfort and satisfaction.

All of the objects—whether rare or commonplace, antique or new—have their place in this made-to-order decor. From the alcove to the side table, everything comes together to form a whole.

The Alps

NESTLING HIGH AMONG THE ALPINE PEAKS AND UPLANDS,
MOUNTAIN HOSPITALITY RELIES ON GOOD FOOD
AND AN UNIMPEACHABLE SENSE OF WELCOME:
SIMPLE YET REFINED; ESSENTIAL AND NATURAL.

AN ALPINE CHALET

It is probably no coincidence that the whole adventure kicked off deep in the heart of the French Alps. Cut off for part of the year, life in the Savoy is tough, and exercising two trades is a common expedient here. Hardship reinforces local beliefs and the feeling of belonging to a family, one of farmers and mountain folk. It is a place that forges the character. Still, to really get to grips with what they have in mind, you have to ascend to their Alpine chalet. At these altitudes, one is closer to a reality that has remained anchored for generations in traditions and local skills. The getaway is well worth it in itself—but this is one escape you'll never forget. The richness, the abundance of Nature are all pervasive. Walking or climbing, one is buoyed up by the surrounding natural beauty. The hours toll on, as if time were suspended.

Walking, climbing, one is carried along by the glorious beauty around. A bracing stroll in the mountain takes about two hours, the silence barely broken by the sound of cowbells in the distance as a herd is driven to upland pastures. A sun-drenched walk though the fir forest, complete with vertical drops, winding paths, and steep climbs, emerges 5,900 feet (1,000 meters) above Megève into a bower where nature once again asserts her rights. In the midst of fields of gentian and wild rhododendron, marmots and capercaillie frolic, and you might even spot the occasional chamois or wild boar that has lost its way.

On arrival, the comfortable chalet sits in well-upholstered simplicity. The Pré Rosset was in the beginning an authentic mountain chalet, a refuge for shepherds on the banks of a little lake with a vista over the Aravis valley and the cirque of the pass at Véry. Such upland refuges were originally barns that sheltered both animals and hayricks. These eminently rustic farmsteads were built by peasants out of timber on a stone base and included a byre. The barn stood above and offered a bare

Megève has preserved the character of an authentic village, and the chalets of the Fermes fit easily into the setting (preceding pages). Decorated with cowbells (facing page), this room opens directly onto the mountainside. The woodwork decor is brightened by a pretty painting unearthed in a secondhand furniture dealer's (above). The chalet's main room is decorated with farmhouse furniture (following pages).

minimum of comfort for staying the night: a bale of hay placed not too far from the stove that kept you warm.

Today the refuge has been transformed. The cattle shed converted into a living space is where more hedonistic hikers meet up in summer and winter alike. The chalet remains much as it was originally. Period architecture with a frontage clad in *ancelles* (wooden shingles that keep the worst of the weather at bay) and covered in roofing stone, with rough flooring. Here too, wood is everywhere, both outside—with the shingle and bolt roof, sloping to prevent the snow lying too thickly—and inside, from ceiling rafters to pale-wood floors. The south-facing windows are small, with frames that fit snugly to cut down the draught. The entrance leads straight into the main living room, with a vast stone and timber fireplace designed by Jean-Louis, ideal for preparing tasty traditional snacks in winter. In this place that evinces a magical charm, the old country furniture seems to have been here forever. The furniture seems to remember the past: the pantry, the Savoyard dressers, and the venerable coffers that serve as seats—all salvaged by the Sibuets—bear time's imprint. The space is structured, however, by the old farm table and the shepherd's bench. Designed to be space saving, the cupboards are embedded in alcoves. The benches too are attached to the walls. Every nook and cranny is made the most of: space has to be earned. Checkered cushions make the wooden settles feel cozy.

Far from the madding crowd, this haven facing the mountain allows time and space for a convivially rustic lunch served on the farmhouse table out on the Pré Rosset wood terrace (below). Before lunch, the hikers recharge their batteries with a spread of country sandwiches (right).

After the excursion there's a refreshing and energizing herb tea, with thyme or *serpolet* and mountain honey. Every hand to the pump is required to prepare the lunch, which comprises regional dishes—rabbit with wild thyme and *crozets* with carrots—together with filling, gourmet salads. In the neat little bedroom on the upper floor, a wooden bed of the traditional type is like a cozy, welcoming nest. The bedrooms bathe in an authentic yet refined simplicity—both the children's with their bunk beds and the parents' that benefits from an intimate feel with their light curtains. The floor is of bare wood, the chairs are straw bottomed. The subtle hues of the bedspreads are played off against the warmer nuances of the wood. The valance takes its cue from a type of box bed that once was a frequent sight in the mountains. The red Vichy curtains bring out the innocent simplicity of period patterns on raw linen. The curtains simply slide along rods like room dividers—the privilege of privacy. At the foot of each bed, there are plaids in case the nights turn chilly. The earthenware jugs and jars hail from the valley as well.

In one corner of the room stands a stove that can heat the whole house if necessary. Cut out of a fir trunk, the hand basin reminds one of a drinking trough, while various handmade articles give the decor a personal touch. There is a pine conserve rack laden with pots of all sizes, and a fir-wood Reblochon drier with doors in whipped wicker. On the credence shelves stand a collection of old painted and enameled metal coffee pots. Adorning the walls are bells that once hung around the necks of cattle so they could be found when lost in fog. Depending on the sound, a shepherd could tell which animal was in difficulties. And then, like a quizzical leitmotif, bears of every conceivable size and shape—in wood of course, but in all kinds of other materials besides—stand on window ledges, between the chandeliers, or lording it on the mantelpiece. When the table is laid, the jute-string table-cloth, square cotton and linen runners printed with edelweiss and the linen napkins decorated with a sprig of fir compose a harmony in plants that chimes in well with the color scheme on the plates.

Reached up a narrow flight of stairs that leads to a corridor giving on the bedrooms and bathrooms, the diminutive openings on the floor above are meant to let in little sunlight. In the old-wood alcoves, a vast pile of plump eiderdowns in country-style fabrics cradles the sleep of the brave, while the checked curtains and coverings in flowery cottons are another of the interior decorator's discreet interventions. Headboards propped up against the walls serve as bedside tables. The space is partitioned by unassuming bolts of plain cloth or *drap de Bonneval*, borrowed from the monks of the region or from some alpine huntsman, and gathered onto a rod; or else a bedspread thrown over a wooden pole. Red gingham too is much in evidence. The bunk beds are set into the wall and hung with woolen curtains. Rough-hewn, worn wooden planks saved from an old grain cupboard were reused to build box beds resembling the traditional models.

The boon of staying high above the plain is that rare luxury of having the mountain all to oneself. There is nothing better, when one climbs a bit and the weather is set fair, than being buoyed along by the scent of aromatic plants billowing through the air. One comes to know how to take in the invigorating, freshly tilled earth, plants dampened by the dew, and the telltale odor of newly mown grass, and to enjoy the sylvan, resinous fragrance of the pine and fir needles. To revel in the tiny blooms that grace the pathway to the

The terrace decking just outside the French windows in the bedroom provides space enough for a table and some deckchairs so one can enjoy the view over the garden (facing page and above).

summit so colorfully. On the way up, the flora is abundant: St John's wort, junipers, melissa, wild celery, or even raspberry cane that, braving the cold, grows quite well at reasonable altitudes. Gentian remains the preeminent mountain plant, though, with its tall, upright stem, its fleshy leaves, and tight, bright yellow flowers. It flourishes here as far as the eye can see. With a little luck, you'll come across beehives that supply a mountain honey heady with the scent of wild flowers, such as the strong-smelling masterwort or hawthorn. For an amateur herbalist, this spectacular site, which has resisted both the assaults of man and the vagaries of time, amounts to a paradise. "With the doggedness of her rural upbringing, my grandmother, Marie, drummed into me a sense and a taste for anything and everything to do with the plants and the soil of our land."

In mountain pastures, the rituals are nourished by customs and folkways which, in former times, appeared with the seasonal transferral of the cattle to highland pastures. At this time the farmers would move up to their summer quarters, where they returned to traditional ways of living that had been handed down from

A nap in the open air with a view over the garden is a pleasure difficult to resist. More decorative than functional, the collection of bird enclosures has grown steadily over the years, and greets visitors as they enter the chalet.

In a bedroom, a daring mix of geometric and colorful forms, with Scottish tartan on the large, more traditional armchair, and two-tone stripes on the contemporary-looking carpet. The ensemble is rounded off with heavy white curtains over the windows. There are mountain motifs on the bed and snowflakes on the rug. The intricate painted-woodwork ceiling is in the purest local tradition.

generation to generation. Today, lunch is the cue for a joyous get-together, unbuttoned, communal. On the climb, children pick wild flowers and thistles that are used to create bucolic decorations. The organization is faultless. The table is laid out on the big terrace, with large plates on the tartan-check tablecloth: a pleasurable, informal meal between companions. Both the standard and the gourmet menus provide ample scope for enjoying the produce of this bountiful land. On occasion, the mountain chalet provides a backdrop to the joys and emotion of a wedding reception … but that's another story. From upland meadow to village chalet, Jocelyne explores every facet of the mountain environment. The warm-hearted comforts typical of mountain living take on more sophisticated forms in each of the zones she has refurbished in Megève. Yet, from the peaceful Coin du Feu to the more worldly Mont Blanc Hotel, via the now legendary Fermes de Marie, in the end what one comes away with is the soul of a place teeming with authenticity and sincerity.

A MOUNTAIN HOME

Let there be no doubt—Jocelyne Sibuet's fief remains Megève, a hard-working, prim little town that lives its life rather differently from elsewhere. Even today, Megève is still a large-sized, tidy and industrious town, rather out of the ordinary. The atmosphere is peculiar, half-upmarket, half-unbuttoned—a curious, unlikely mix of the chic and the rustic. Timeless period images, souvenir photos, postcards almost imprinted on the collective memory ... a picture in one's mind's eye of the classic traditional mountain chalet, half buried under a hoary cloak of snowflakes.... Seductive and dashing, the archetype of the fashionable ski resort, in its prime Megève hit the silver screen, and fueled many a poet and many a saga. As ever, it was Jean Cocteau who came up with the oft-repeated quip: "Megève, Paris's twenty-first arrondissement." Megève seems to be a place wreathed in smiles that flirts with evasion and vacation.

In spite of appearances, however, Megève is at heart a real Savoy village, with all the warmth of a rural hamlet, human in size, where age-old traditions remain very much alive; a preserve that supports still-active farms. At a young age, Jocelyne Sibuet absorbed all she could from the energy of these highlands, imbued by unalterable values combined with a curiosity for all things modern. The country child drank in its good sense and its fondness for truth, for noble and living materials. Though ever on the move, she soon understood she could never live for long away from this mountain retreat and its essential ingredient, its heart and soul, its wide-open spaces. In the midst of the fir trees and the fast-flowing highland streams, the bubbling springs and rocky cascades, in the life-enhancing air and amid mineral energies, she could ground herself, recharge her batteries. It was there, in this bastion of nature, that the history of the Compagnie des Hôtels de Montagne saw the light of day under the majestic wing of the Mont Blanc. Can one imagine a more awe-inspiring backdrop?

"We did what we've done because we wanted to fulfill the desires of a public vainly yearning for locations with soul, with roots, with traditions; a rural feel, a history. Les Fermes correspond to this craving for authenticity, this ideal of serenity, of living comfortably with one's family and friends. Group and individual. These chalets,

A row of mountain stones, laid beneath the overhanging eaves, covers a space where grass would never grow due to the lack of light. Openings to the outside and natural vistas have always been uppermost in the mind of the lady of the house. A small worktable is always set before the window so you can just sit and enjoy the spectacle.

this village within a village we've built, conveys our past as well as our hopes, though one can feel at home there whatever one's origin."

A tiny hamlet within a small town, Les Fermes de Marie stand in two hectares of parkland in the heart of Megève, and offer a prime example of the true spirit of Haute Savoy. The farms, woods, antiquities, crafts, and cooking all embody the life and culture of these mountains: a high-grown style and period that never loses its sense of proportion and that respects tradition—yet it is a tradition that has been improved, updated. At one time, the inhabitants of Alpine zones could only survive thanks to the mountain. This was a dependency that reflected itself in their dwelling places. The forest used to be a source of income and of a highly developed craft tradition. A priceless raw material, wood, lined homes inside and out alike. It was used to make roof frames and to panel walls and ceilings. Chalets were low-slung so as to guard against extremes of temperature. Today too, the form of the chalet echoes a yearning for reassurance, a striving for quality. And, ever faithful to itself in terms of material and trim, it has proved a bastion against the pernicious effects of vulgarization. "I was born into the trade. I quickly became acquainted with the laws of hotel management, with the concept of service, with a convivial environment—and with the heat of a large kitchen." And very soon, Jocelyne was getting her hands dirty, heading up her first hotel, Le Coin du Feu, at twenty-one. Over her ten-year stint, she got to grips with the realities of administration, with the demands of day-to-day management. She learnt how to receive guests. Her training was clearly no picnic, and, if it left its mark, it also gave her confidence, especially when she had a home to run and two young children, Nicolas and Marie, to bring up as well.

A turning point in the history of the business came in 1989, with the public opening of the Fermes de Marie and the changes in lifestyle this involved. Knowing how to restore implies a particular expertise that is expressed to the full here. Before building his own, Jean-Louis Sibuet spent almost ten years buying up long-abandoned farms—more than fifty, as well as barns, sheepfolds, haylofts, and cattle sheds, accumulating, as he puts it, "piles of wood" that he was to rehabilitate as building material.

"Every chunk of wood has a story to tell, and every farmer told me this story," Jean-Louis recalls. At that time, he made a point of only pulling down farms that had collapsed or infringed planning regulations,

Wood dominates the decoration, outside and in. Here, at the entrance to the Fermes, it rubs shoulders with stonework. The bench, made to measure by a local craftsman, adds a note of comfort to the open space and ensures that hikers can make those final preparations before setting off for the mountains.

In the dining room in one of the chalets, where traditional reds and greens predominate, the rugs mix Indian and Scottish patterns. Meanwhile, an unpretentious carved wooden rosette speaks of its Tarentais origins. With a wink to the visitor, candleholders—of more recent make—here bear a second glance. Getting different styles to live together in harmony is one of Jocelyne's favorite occupations. Between the carved Savoy furniture, the tall standard lamps, the armchair, and the carpets of different styles and periods, the coherence is obvious. Here too, objects are juxtaposed, upsetting one another, shaking one another up. Tirelessly, Jocelyne scours the world, amassing objects. With each trip, her collection of souvenirs, whose inventory would surely have enchanted French poet Jacques Prévert, swells. A propeller, a carving of a bear, a pair of antediluvian skis, hunting trophies, old-fashioned fishing equipment, bamboo canes, superannuated winches, classic hand-painted lures, naive paintings ... all get on swimmingly, lying about here and there, affixed to walls or placed, as if forgotten, in niches or in an eighteenth-century fir-wood armoire. In this way she recreates the kind of natural accretion one finds in those family houses where generation after generation have spent their holidays.

From the washbasin rough hewn out of a great tree trunk, to the bathtub dressed in timber billets, wood is equally at home in the bathrooms. These are a continuation of the bedrooms, almost forming part of them, in a rustic or sophisticated harmony. Hunting trophies naturally find a home there, too. The stool legs even sport deer hooves. Country furniture provides an authentic note. The multitude of cushions and the soft, yielding plaids slipped over the foot of the bed add a touch of gentleness and comfort.

thus saving them for a new life somewhere else. Some had been with us for more than three hundred years: recycling them gave them a second chance. All this wood, which might have been burned in fireplaces and reduced to ashes, ended up as timber frames. These provide Les Fermes de Marie with the perennial grace of a Savoy village, albeit on a reduced scale, and laid the foundations of a project motivated by a raison d'être, a coherence. "One cannot design this sort of village and then throw it down just anywhere." Jean-Louis also evokes elements such as simplicity and necessity, just as in times past, when each space corresponded to a purpose. He never loses sight of the fact that whatever has little or no function in a house cannot last long. The quality of old buildings derives from a perfect mastery over techniques that is calculated to maximize longevity. Still today, these objective values reflect convenience and authenticity, even an aesthetic. Purity of form, sobriety, lack of pretension. And criteria such as naturalness, comfort, and solidity.

Like many a Savoyard worth his salt, Jocelyne's great-grandfather was one of the so-called "red collars" at Drouot's, the Paris auction house. Life in the family home unfolded among antique furniture and local produce—in particular in the kitchen, the beating heart of the family. The vague scent of wax polish floated in the air, and with it the pleasure of growing up constantly surrounded by unusual, costly objects of every provenance and from every period: Baroque and Henri IV, Gallé faience vases or bronzes. Early on, Jocelyne showed herself receptive to pieces of quality. Almost unconsciously, she learnt all the subtleties, all the nuances of the style between the valleys of the Tarentaise and the Maurienne; these make for the richness of a rosette or the symbolism of the heart that frequently adorns Savoyard folk furniture. It is a motif often found carved on wooden trunks, tables, alcove beds, and on wedding armoires. "For me, folk art evinces simplicity, sensitivity, the patience of whoever made the piece, sometimes clumsily, but always with heart and with passion." Coincidentally, Jocelyne also acquired a thorough knowledge of Jacques Henri Lemesne, an important figure from the years 1940 to 1950, whose work has since become a benchmark. His impact was especially significant at a time when, totally unexpectedly, substantial buildings began to spring up in the mountains. His purist style and rigor are only today being rediscovered. This early initiation was not to go unrewarded. Objects are a genuine passion for her, and combing the secondhand stores remains one of Jocelyne's greatest joys. At twenty-one

Here, birchwood gives the illusion of a forest; there, sequoia or cherry beams and logs; farther on, plum-wood effects. Wood is worked every which way; wood is king. Even the stag's head is carved out of a piece of timber.

it is hard to be very assured of one's tastes and one takes comfort in either greater simplicity or in playfulness; but over time, needless to say, one develops. "Of course, I can't see myself being responsible for a Zen interior, for one in unreconstructed design. It doesn't make me feel comfortable, even if my tastes have become more assertive and even if at the moment I am moving towards a more purist spirit." With the passing of the years, though, you acquire an education, you adapt to the environment, to the zeitgeist. You forge your own personality; your road becomes surer, more personal. The important thing is to travel one's own path in a number of styles. Self-questioning is an occupational hazard, but, with hindsight, you understand that your roots, your expectations never change, that you always plow the same furrow. "I know I will always be looking for ample spaces, for the lamp that gives the most beautiful light; that I will always be hunting down that detail, that accessory which brings life into a house—be it a table, a bouquet, a scent…." Tiny things that melt into the whole, but which, arranged one beside the other, participate in the overall effect, and that influence—determine even—the first impression. Invisible details that can switch "I don't like that" into "I like that."

The contrast between wood and pebbling is accentuated around the fireplace to create a more imposing atmosphere. To bring out the surround made of polished round glacier stones, new furniture was constructed, including a few pieces made of antler. Tree-trunk tables fall in with chairs made of branches, log shelving, and other furnishings of generous proportions—benches, sideboards, trunks…. And from tartan to plain shades, the whole conspires to create a warm-hearted feel.

THE AUTHENTICITY
OF WOOD

Houses live, show signs of age, of wear and tear. Here, everything is taken apart and rebuilt. It cannot be denied that some printed textiles fall out of fashion sooner than others, that certain fabrics date and age badly. When this becomes obvious, then urgent change is called for, and no regret should be felt. The essence is to remain aware, and to be prepared to tack so as to remain on course. And, because one should never let a house look drab, for their fifteen-year anniversary recently, Les Fermes enjoyed a lick of paint. The bedrock has not budged an inch. Les Fermes consist of chalets in seasoned timber, spacious bedrooms, and small private terraces from where one can gaze out over the mountaintops. There is no question of abandoning the warm style and the collection of old furniture.

Previously, wood had not quite finished revealing its hidden treasures—now it's in its prime. Rough, raw materials are more than ever in evidence. Stone and granite gain in importance. Some walls have been altered and new spaces created. The original bathrooms have been overhauled and now offer every hi-tech convenience. The regeneration has been total. It expresses a desire, as it were, to transform what existed before only so as to complete it, to finish it off—the summit of sophistication. Such a duty of care makes a house blossom. But it is essential to remain permanently vigilant and keep adapting those vital areas, even if there is no need to do anything, even if there is nothing to replace or renew. Similarly, it is best first to simply absorb, without any particular purpose in mind, to drink in the atmosphere, to just look around. Simply collecting information and seeing the latest fads allows one's desires to take root, so that later on one can make surer, less awkward choices. Moreover, taking the time to reflect makes one impervious to untimely impulses, to temptations best resisted. For Jocelyne, traveling up to Paris means doing the rounds of the showrooms. "I'll go and see my favorite textile manufacturers, getting an idea of the prints, of the colors that accord with my personal palette and which I really like. I know that, one day, I will find them a place, somewhere or other." When she started out she was scarcely able to visit the capital without—between two appointments—making a beeline for the Marché St-Pierre to replenish her stock of fabrics. She chose unusual and classic fabrics —tweeds and tartans for gents' suits, for example—which she took malicious pleasure in hijacking for interiors.

The balcony overlooks the village: To take breakfast out there, watch over the village as it wakes up, and to drink in the beams of the rising sun, is one of the first pleasures of the day. The plain wood table and armchairs were specially made for outside use. More sophisticated, the large Savoyard clock forms a pendant with the hunting trophy, the chandeliers, and the original carved furniture to create a refined backdrop.

Mountain style for the main room; it is a good ruse to head here come lunchtime…. The main piece of furniture was made in the traditional manner from an original design by Jean-Louis Sibuet. The chairs are Tyrolean in inspiration. The table setting in the dining room has a more sophisticated, hunting look. Bordeaux table linen and an old chair made of antler covered in bronze-colored velvet create stunning color contrasts. On the log-lined walls, black-and-white photographs from the 1950s celebrate the mountain and the beginnings of winter sports.

Untreated, polished, sophisticated, elegant: on each of the company's sites at Megève, wood reigns supreme. It is omnipresent, from the pine-cone paneling to the hazel-wood ceiling. There are more than ten varieties of timber here. On floors it ages gracefully and, far from suffering with the years, acquires a patina. Bringing with it all the tranquil strength of nature, and even a certain spirituality, this eminently malleable material is subjected to every possible treatment and explored in all its many states. It is cut into billets, discs, sections, boards, or kept just as it is to emphasize the relief of veins that catch the light so harmoniously. Birch is used to provide an illusion of the forest, along with great disks of sequoia or cherry, and, farther off, plum wood. Sober and functional in furniture, it recedes into the decor, as witness the hand basins dug out of tree trunks, the wooden couches designed by Jean Louis Sibuet, and the huge carved armoires.

Wood acquires still finer values next to such muscular foils as stone and granite, polished balls of glacier rock, the corners smoothed down by the violence of the rushing waters, the sheer force of the raging torrent. In conjunction, they weave a

natural and comfortable decor, as does soft, giving, warm cashmere, an ideal material for cuddling up to in the long winters. All diffuse the organicity, the nobility of fine raw materials, and distill that absolute, that incomparable refinement that fosters pleasure and well-being.

In the chalets, the fireplace is designed as a focal point. It is at the fireside, around the wood crackling in the hearth and the logs that snap and explode, that the family gathers, that friends meet up, that stories are told. It is there one seeks warmth when the cold starts to bite hard. It is the fireplace that provides the rhythm for the heart and life of the house. It illuminates and brings comfort in the storm or in the silence of the refuge or mountain hideaway. There, one roasts sweet chestnuts, lights candles and incense with a calming scent. Through it waft fragrances that are impossible to forget: the authentic odor of the house. "Each place has its corresponding smell. In the mountains, a house is permeated by fragrances of various kinds of wood, by the scent of the fire in the hearth." And in saying that Jocelyne Sibuet reveals the powerful talent of someone in the vanguard, of one who dares to mix things up. Pine, fir, wax, spices, essential oils…. To possess a nose for such things is a requirement as well as a genuine talent. Marrying different periods and mixing materials is one of Jocelyne's great fortes, and she adores unexpected contrasts. Fusing English, Austrian, and Savoyard trends might appear risky, but the end result is far more rewarding and intriguing than sticking to the straight and narrow. Daring juxtapositions of plain sectioned wood, tartan, and weathered leather can set up teasing and novel optical effects, winning combinations. In this revised and corrected version of "home sweet home," the ever-so-traditional tweed suiting for men, or denim for fashion jeans and outfits, become impressively natural coverings on cushions scattered around the fireplace, insolently rubbing shoulders with stripes that scuttle over the carpet, armchairs, and couch. They stand out strongly, gaining depth in comparison with the broad expanses of plain walls. It is a subtle, fragile balance that is built up with each passing day, thanks to some piece of old English furniture or a hundred-year-old Savoy dresser, locally produced textiles and imported accessories. So objects too can be juxtaposed, can upset and shake one another up. Tirelessly, she combs the world, amassing objects and enriching her collection with souvenirs from each journey. A propeller, a carving of a bear, a pair of antediluvian skis, hunting trophies, old-fashioned fishing equipment,

In the main drawing room, a pause for hot chocolate with cinnamon in the enveloping comfort of its voluptuous sofas. The fresco—signed Jean Cocteau—in one of the salons next door has inspired an interior right out of the poet's world, or off the set of one of his famous films. The errant angels seem to turn an indulgent eye on events in this little world.

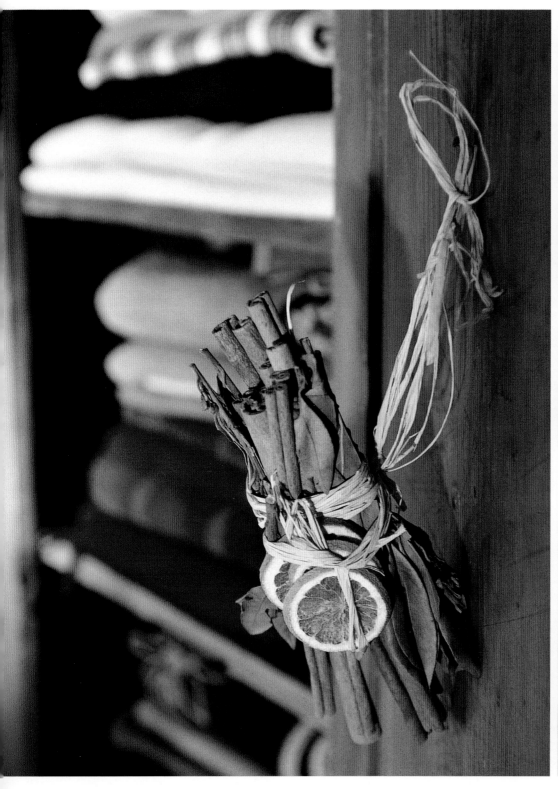

bamboo canes, superannuated winches, old hand-painted lures, naive paintings … all cohabit perfectly well, lying about here and there or affixed to walls or deliberately forgotten in niches along the corridors or on the side tables. Yet this riot is always gently kept in check, since the essential point is to ensure the space remains cozy, comfortable, and convivial—and full of light. In the mountains, one's relationship to the sun is not the same as on the plain. You often have to lean out of a window to follow the sun's path as it goes down. A pity this, since the colors of the winter sky—pink, mauve, and midnight blue—afford such beautiful harmonies, unfailing pleasure to the eye. When she returns to her brushes and palette, savage, burning nature is an inspiration to Jocelyne. She adores reinterpreting all she finds in a naive style. Discreetly, here and there along the corridors and in the sitting rooms in Les Fermes, there hang little pictures showing village houses under snow, or farmland, or harvest time. Lacking some of the advantages of the plain, there are still many enjoyable sensations to be had in the course of the day. Here, then, it is the natural elements that dictate the rules. Except during the summer months, people don't venture outside so much, preferring a quiet life indoors where they can retreat into themselves.

So Jocelyne Sibuet approaches every project like a novelist weaving the threads of a plot. The mood up in the mountains is geared to simplicity: nature, the soil, and traditions provide all the sources she needs to draw on. Refinements come later in the shape of an object, an accessory, a tiny detail—a candle, for example, whose flame softens the rugged authenticity of the natural materials, adding a glimmer of mystery. The omnipresence of wood preserves the sense of intimacy. In Megève, when fitting out the location as a series of variations on a theme, Jocelyne manages to respect the personality of each zone. Flagstones, visibly more than two hundred years old and recovered from ancient castles in the region, provide tonal warmth to the vast main room of Les Fermes. One can also find stacks of old pottery, as well as an enormous cheese press boasting at least a century's active service, and ancient timber door panels remounted as wainscoting.

In the cupboards in the chalet, cinnamon-orange fagots mix adorably with the smell of fir. This time it is the mix of materials—tartan and flannel—that adds warmth to this quietly unpretentious bedroom. The Bonneval cloth, traditional in the region, and fake fur take the chill off the bed (preceding double page). Old pieces of furniture—here, a period secrétaire or Austrian chest of drawers, flannel, hessian, and plaids—give a classier touch to the traditional rustic. A rebuilt baldachin, a Savoyard trunk at the foot of the bed, wooden flooring, carved lamp, choice accessories and prints on the wall, a kingsize percale duvet, cushions and plaids, bunches of flowers and seasonal fruits: these are details that guarantee tender moments snuggled in a mountain cocoon.

THE ESSENCE
OF CELEBRATION

Midnight supper on Christmas Eve in the mountains is a time to cherish, an exceptional celebration for which no expense is spared. It is a precious time, even slightly mystical when linked to the tales and dreams of childhood. And the feathery bubbles of champagne, like living symbols of the party, sparkle on: it is best drunk with ripe, blood-red strawberries. Every year, on Christmas Eve, when the brightly lit scene is accompanied by stunning taste sensations, delight is afforded by the tiniest things. For in the end, it is only when all the details come together that a party goes with a swing. Throwing the clichés out of the window, red and green are in abundance as is traditional in the uplands. Taffeta and linen tablecloths, crystal chandeliers and antler cutlery add to the effect. But, juxtaposed with the transparent crystal, the Baroque gilt also has panache. The white cloth on the table and the ecru cotton underscore the neutral tone and the vigor of natural wood. Then there is the magical, wintry sophistication of the majestic branches of fir. The main thing, though, is that the songs of good cheer be rendered with conviction. Tassels, drops, stars, baroque glassware, blown-glass pendants, and ruddy apples; mountain crystal that glitters and glints differently depending on the light. The hanging decorations must be carefully chosen and varied in accordance with the years and the captain's mood. Candles and bouquets are dressed in the brightest coats.

The guest of honor is the soft and downy edelweiss, the snowy immortelle, flower of the glaciers. Rare, precious, it deserves star billing. This tiny but amazing flower seems to encapsulate all the life force of our mountain flora and Les Fermes have crowned her Queen. A snowman and a fir tree, centerpieces of any self-respecting Christmas, are compulsory. And, especially if the feast is accompanied by powdery snowflakes that crystallize as the midnight peel sounds, the guests can hardly fail to be of good cheer.

The key lies in the table setting. As Jocelyne declares: "Giving pleasure as a hostess is something I find richly rewarding. It brings out still more the idea of sharing, of interchange, which for me is the real driving force. All this bustling around fills

As day turns to evening, twinkling nightlights show the way to the fireside. In the mountains, Christmas is still a very special event. Megève preserves its inimitable charm beneath a snowy cloak, especially when one can still soak up the sun on the terrace.

BELOW AND FACING PAGE:

Every detail counts when preparing for Christmas festivities.
It is a precious time; a time outside time in the silence of the
white-clad village that upholds its traditions and respects the soul
of the mountain. There is nothing better than mulled wine to warm
one up after a long day's skiing or a snowball fight. Once their dog
tires of blazing the trail, hikers tramp from one chalet to another
and find refuge around the fireplace for a moment's peace.

PAGES 56–57:

The traditional Christmas colors of red and green are used to
deck out the fir tree and its decorations, right down to the dishes
laden with red fruits *en gelée*. The decorations are unpretentious,
from a stylized roly-poly Santa to a paper chain. Powdery snow, a
view over the terrace by candlelight—the seductive mystery
remains intact.

me with a kind of lightheartedness, since, if to be a good hostess is part of our daily
code of conduct, then it is joyously confirmed by the exceptional. A beautifully laid
table over which time is taken, so as to share a moment of closeness with one's
family or companions, is a real delight to me. When we set the table for a simple
birthday, it is exactly the same thing." And she indulges in the shimmering depth of
hunting decor, with its gamut of rich hues (Bordeaux, chestnut, chocolate), and all
the subtle nuances of brown or auburn tones or dark reds. To enhance the sense of
occasion, she will dot about little candles whose bright souls are reflected in the
color and transparency of a crystal glass, great baskets of walnuts and hazelnuts
that will later be unceremoniously plundered, oranges pricked with cloves, cinnamon sticks. And then, in small doses, spices, pinecones, gold and silver balls. The
Baroque with its intricate forms, its trenchant colors, its parade of gold, can tolerate
a hint of excess and quiet madness. It brings color and life to wherever one feels at
ease. "This universe of angels, of gilt, of dazzling colors does much to sustain the
dream." And if one night above all others summons forth a dreamworld, it surely
must be Christmas Eve....

Christmas: white with variations in gold—the decor is neatly poised between transparency and hints of Baroque. The festivities are prepared meticulously, the harmonies emerging from the details. Candles and bouquets are drenched in light and the Christmas decorations hover, all translucency and weightlessness. Whatever the chosen theme, the table is laid with rustic yet sophisticated naturalness. Bohemian glassware and white porcelain plates rub shoulders with powdered flakes, balls, and the night-lights that enliven the table.

CHRISTMAS RECIPES

CHESTNUT SOUP

SERVES 6–8

INGREDIENTS: 1lb 2 oz (500 g) chestnuts, peeled and parboiled - 2 cups (1/2 liter) veal or chicken broth - 1 quart (1 liter) light cream - Salt and pepper - 2 tsp (10 g) truffles

Heat the broth with the cream. Add the chestnuts, reserving a few for the garnish. Season with salt and pepper. Serve the soup with the reserved chestnuts chopped into pieces and slices of truffle.

SAUTÉED DUCK FOIE GRAS

SERVES 4

INGREDIENTS: 1lb (450 g) foie gras in one piece - 3 1/2 oz (100 g) chestnuts, peeled and parboiled - Salt and pepper

Sauté the foie gras in a frying pan. When it is cooked and has a nice golden color all over, cut it through the center, and fill with the chestnuts. Wrap the foie gras tightly in plastic wrap and leave in the refrigerator for two days. Serve in thin slices.

ROAST TURKEY WITH DRIED FRUIT COMPOTE IN HONEY

SERVES 8–10

INGREDIENTS: 3lb 5 oz (1.5 kg) turkey - 1 3/4 oz (50 g) figs - 1 3/4 oz (50 g) dried pears - 1 3/4 oz (50 g) dried peaches - 1 3/4 oz (50 g) prunes - 1 3/4 oz (50 g) raisins - 2/3 cup (150 g) honey - 1 lemon, juice squeezed - 4 tsp (20 ml) water

Roast the turkey. Meanwhile, heat the honey in a saucepan. Slice all the fruits thinly and place in the top half of a double boiler. Cover with the warm honey, then add the lemon juice and the water. Heat this mixture in the double boiler. Serve the roast turkey accompanied by this compote.

BRANDIED RASPBERRIES

TO MAKE 1 JAR

INGREDIENTS: 2 1/4 lb (1 kg) raspberries - 1 3/4 cups (400 g) sugar - 1 3/4 cups (400 ml) raspberry brandy

Rinse and drain the raspberries. Fill a preserving jar with the raspberries and cover with the sugar and the raspberry brandy. Seal the pot and leave it for 30 days before eating.

BERRY JELLO

INGREDIENTS: 10 1/2 oz (300 g) blueberries - 10 1/2 oz (300 g) strawberries - 10 1/2 oz (300 g) raspberries - 1 quart (1 liter) Domaine de Marie red wine - 2 cups (500 ml) water - 2 3/4 cups (700 g) sugar - 1 tbs unflavored gelatin

Heat the wine and water, add the gelatin, and bring to just below boiling point. Do not let it boil. Take off heat and leave to cool slightly. Place the fruits in a large jar and cover with the mixture of wine and gelatin.

CHRISTMAS STARS

INGREDIENTS: 2 cups (225 g) all-purpose flour, sifted - 1 tsp baking powder - 2 tsp powdered ginger - 1 tsp ground cinnamon - 2 tbs (50 g) butter - 2 tbs maple syrup - 2 tbs (50 g) sugar - 1/2 cup (115 g) confectioner's sugar, sifted

Preheat the oven to 375°F/180°C.
Heat the butter and maple syrup in a double boiler or bain-marie.
Combine the flour, baking powder, sugar, confectioner's sugar, ginger, and cinnamon.
Add the melted butter and maple syrup.
Knead into a firm dough.
Roll out the dough and cut out stars with a cookie cutter.
Arrange the stars on a cookie sheet and bake for 10–12 minutes.

CHRISTMAS RECIPES

MONT BLANC

SERVES 8–10

FOR THE SPONGE CAKE
4 eggs
$^1/_2$ cup (125 g) sugar
1 cup (125 g) all-purpose flour
1 tsp butter

FOR THE CHESTNUT MOUSSE
1 vanilla pod
1 cup (250 ml) milk
4 egg yolks
$^2/_3$ cup (83 g) superfine sugar
1 tbs unflavored gelatin,
    softened in 1 tbs water
$3^1/_2$ oz (100 g) chestnut purée
$2^3/_4$ oz (80 g) marrons glacés,
    broken into pieces
1 cup (250 ml) light cream

WHITE CHOCOLATE MOUSSE
1 cup (250 ml) whipping
    cream
4 squares (125 g) white
    chocolate

ITALIAN MERINGUE
$^2/_3$ cup (150 g) egg whites
$10^1/_2$ oz (300 g) granulated
    sugar
Pinch of confectioner's sugar

UTENSIL
1 bombe mold

TO MAKE THE SPONGE CAKE, put the sugar into a metal bowl, break the eggs over it, and whisk to combine. Place the bowl over boiling water and beat with an electric whisk on high speed for 1 minute. Remove from the heat and continue beating on low speed for 5 minutes. The mixture should be smooth and foaming. Sift the flour and fold it in with a spatula. Pour into a round buttered cake pan and cook on medium heat (350°F/175°C) for about 30 minutes. Unmold the cake while still warm onto a cake rack, and leave to cool completely before slicing it crosswise into four, using a saw-bladed knife.

TO MAKE THE CHESTNUT MOUSSE. Split the vanilla pod lengthwise and put it in a saucepan. Add the milk and bring to the boil. Beat the egg yolks and sugar in a bowl. Pour the boiling milk over them while beating continuously. Pour the mixture into a saucepan and simmer, beating continuously, until it coats the back of a spoon. Remove from the heat and allow to cool slightly before stirring in the softened gelatin. Stir in the chestnut purée and pieces of marrons glacés.

TO MAKE THE WHITE CHOCOLATE MOUSSE. Whip the cream. Break the white chocolate into a bowl standing in hot water. Let it melt slowly. Mix with the whipped cream.

TO ASSEMBLE THE MONT BLANC. Pour a layer of chestnut mousse into the bombe mold. Cover with a round of sponge cake, then spread with a layer of white chocolate mousse, cover with another round of the cake, then add a layer of white chocolate mousse, then a layer of chestnut mousse, and finish with the last round of cake. Refrigerate or, better still, freeze the cake for several hours; it will unmold more easily from frozen.

ITALIAN MERINGUE. Put the sugar into a saucepan with 8 tbs water. Place it on the heat and cook for about 5 minutes or to the firm ball stage (when a drop of syrup will form a ball in a glass of water, 244–248°F/118–120°C on a candy thermometer). Meanwhile, beat the egg whites as stiffly as possible, incorporating the pinch of confectioner's sugar halfway through the process. Pour the boiling syrup over the egg whites very quickly between the sides of the bowl and the whisk. Whisk on low speed until the mixture has cooled completely (about 10 minutes).

Unmold the mousse cake onto a serving platter, and use a spatula to spread it with the meringue. Serve chilled.

LUNCH IN THE ALPINE FOOTHILLS

COLD NETTLE AND HERB SOUP

SERVES 8–10

INGREDIENTS: 1 lb 2 oz (500 g) leeks - 2¹/₄ lb (1 kg) potatoes - 1 bunch young nettle shoots - 1 cup (250 ml) light cream - A handful of each the following herbs: chervil, tarragon, fennel, flat-leaved parsley, chives, coriander - Salt and pepper

Fill a deep pot with 6 cups (1.5 liter) water and boil the potatoes, leeks and nettles for 20 to 30 minutes. Leave to cool at the end of the cooking time. When cold, mix the soup with the herbs and add the light cream. Season before serving.

OPEN-FACED SANDWICHES

Slices of wholewheat bread, toasted and covered with a slice of Savoyard ham, a tablespoon of crushed Serac soft goat cheese or 4 tsp (20 g) of Tomme de Savoie goat-milk or cow's-milk cheese and a tablespoon of chopped chives.

CROZETS WITH CARROTS

SERVES 5

INGREDIENTS: 7 oz (200 g) carrots - 1 cup (250 g) crozets (buckwheat flour noodles, a Savoyard specialty) - 2 quarts (2 liters) chicken stock - Knob of butter for frying - Chopped garlic - Coarse salt - Flat-leaved parsley

Cut the carrots into diamond shapes and boil in salted water. When cooked, rinse under cold running water.
Boil the crozets in the chicken stock for 10 minutes, then drain.
Fry the carrots and crozets together in a frying pan with a little butter, add a little chopped garlic, and deglaze by adding the meat stock and stirring well to dislodge any bits that have stuck to the bottom. Season with salt and pepper and add a handful of flat-leaved parsley.

RABBIT WITH WILD THYME

SERVES 6

INGREDIENTS: 6 rabbit thighs - ¹/₃ cup (100 ml) olive oil - 2³/₄ oz (75 g) butter - 7 oz (200 g) onions - 3¹/₂ oz (100 g) shallots - 2 oz (50 g) garlic - 3¹/₂ oz (100 g) carrots - 3¹/₂ oz (100 g) leeks, green parts only - 1 bunch wild thyme - 2 quarts (2 liters) beef or veal stock - Salt and pepper

Preheat the oven to 375°F/180°C.
Heat the olive oil in a frying pan and sauté the rabbit thighs until they change color.
Meanwhile, melt the butter and fry the onions, garlic, and shallots gently on a low heat. Then add the carrots, green leek parts, and wild thyme.
Pour all these ingredients as well as the stock into a casserole dish and add the rabbit. Season to taste. Bake for around 35 minutes.

BERTHOUD

SERVES I

INGREDIENTS: 7 oz (200 g) Abondance cheese cut into slices (Abondance is a dry cow's-milk cheese available in good delicatessens) - 2 cups (500 ml) dry white wine - 2 tsp (10 ml) madeira - Chopped garlic- Pepper

Put all the ingredients into a gratin dish. Bake for 15 minutes in a preheated 375°F (180°C) oven.

BLUEBERRY TART

SERVES 6–8

INGREDIENTS: 8 oz (250 g) shortcrust dough - 1³/₄ cups (400 g) blueberries - ¹/₃ cup (100 ml) blackcurrant jelly glaze

Preheat the oven to 375°F (180°C). Roll out the dough and use it to line a buttered tart pan. To prevent the base rising when it cooks, cover it with parchment paper and dried beans or baking beans. Bake the shortcrust for 15 minutes. Heat the jelly glaze in a saucepan and mix it with the blueberries. Fill the tart with the blueberry mixture.

DINNER IN THE CHALET

PUMPKIN, BACON, AND TRUFFLE SOUP

SERVES 6

INGREDIENTS: 1 small pumpkin weighing approx. 6$^{1}/_{2}$ lb (3 kg) - 2 tbs (50 g) butter - 3$^{1}/_{2}$ oz (100 g) onions - 4 cups (1 liter) chicken stock - 1 lb (450 g) salted pork belly, in one piece - 1 bouquet garni - $^{3}/_{4}$ oz (20 g) truffles

Slice the pumpkin in half, peel it and scoop out the seeds. Heat the butter in a deep saucepan with a lid, add the chunks of pumpkin flesh and onions, and cook on low heat. Cover with the stock and simmer for 90 minutes. When cooked, purée in a food processor.
Meanwhile, boil the pork belly with a bouquet garni (thyme, bay leaf, leek, parsley) for 90 minutes.
Leave to cool.
Cut the meat into cubes and serve with the soup, which should be sprinkled with truffle shavings.

POLENTA SQUARE

SERVES 2

INGREDIENTS: 3$^{1}/_{2}$ cups (500 g) yellow cornmeal - 3 cups (750 ml) milk - 3 cups (750 ml) water - Salt and pepper - Pinch of grated nutmeg - 4 tbs (60 ml) heavy cream

Boil the yellow cornmeal in the milk and water for 30 minutes. Drain, season with salt and pepper, and add nutmeg.
Pour the cooked cornmeal into a dish and incorporate the cream.
Leave for 10 minutes before serving.

VANILLA PEARS IN SYRUP

SERVES 6

INGREDIENTS: 6 pears - 2 cups (500 g) sugar - 1 quart (1 liter) water - 2 vanilla pods

Pour the sugar, water, and vanilla into a saucepan and cook on low heat for 20 minutes to produce a syrup.
Poach the pears in the syrup, on very gentle heat, without allowing them to boil.
Remove from the heat, leave to cool, then chill.
Serve the pears in the syrup.

MULLED WINE

SERVES 6

INGREDIENTS: 2 cups (500 ml) red wine - $^{1}/_{3}$ cup (100 ml) Grand Marnier - $^{1}/_{3}$ cup (100 ml) Cointreau - $^{1}/_{3}$ cup (100 ml) Curaçao - $^{1}/_{3}$ cup (100 g) brown sugar - 1 cinnamon stick - 1 clove - 1 orange segment - 1 lemon segment

Combine all the ingredients in a large deep pot. As soon the liquid starts to "shiver," remove from the heat and serve immediately.

Dinner in the Chalet

Shoulder of Veal with Porcini

SERVES 8

INGREDIENTS: 2^1/$_4$ lb (1 kg) shoulder of veal - 1 quart (1 liter) veal stock - 2^1/$_4$ lb (1 kg) porcini mushrooms - 1 bouquet garni - 2 thyme sprigs - Salt and pepper

FOR THE POLENTA: ^{2}/$_3$ cup (100 g) yellow polenta - 7 tbs (100 ml) heavy cream - 8 fl oz (250 ml) milk - Salt and pepper

Preheat the oven to 325°F/180°C. Roast the veal for 45 minutes, basting with the veal stock from time to time. Add the bouquet garni and the thyme. Meanwhile clean the porcini, washing them quickly in water without allowing them to become waterlogged. Cut them into pieces and sauté briefly so that they give up their liquid. Reserve them. Cook the polenta in the milk and cream. Pour the cooked polenta into a jelly-roll pan (high-sided cookie sheet) and leave to cool. When cool, use a circular cookie cutter to cut it into rounds. Melt a little butter and sauté the polenta rounds until golden on both sides. At the same time, sauté the porcini in another frying pan. Serve the shoulder of veal with the polenta rounds and the porcini.

This recipe is traditionally made with shoulder of pork, as shown in the photograph.

Risotto

SERVES 6

INGREDIENTS: 7 oz (200 g) Arborio rice - 2 tbs olive oil - 2 shallots - 1 tsp sea salt - 2 cups (450 ml) chicken or veal stock - ^{1}/$_3$ cup (100 g) Parmesan, grated - 5 tbs (80 g) butter - Salt

Heat the oil in a deep frying pan or wide-based saucepan.
Add the shallots, rice, and salt. Fry for 3 minutes. Gradually add the stock, stirring with a spatula. Cook for 15–20 minutes. At the end of the cooking time, add the parmesan, butter, and sea salt.

Bugnes (Kindling Cookies)

SERVES 10

INGREDIENTS: 4 cups (500 g) all-purpose flour - ^{2}/$_3$ cup (150–200 g) sugar - 2 whole eggs or 6 yolks - 2 tsp (10 g) baking powder - 1 tsp (5 g) salt - 2^1/$_2$ tablespoons (50 ml) rum - 2 tsp (10 g) vanilla sugar - Grated rind of 1 lemon - Sugar for sprinkling

Sift the flour and add the sugar, eggs, baking powder, softened butter, and then the rest of the ingredients, excluding the sugar for sprinkling. Knead into a dough. Wrap in plastic wrap and refrigerate overnight.
The next day, roll out the dough on a floured surface to a thickness of ^{1}/$_8$ inch (3 mm). Cut it into 4-inch (10-cm) strips measuring 1^1/$_2$ inches (4 cm) wide. Cut a slit in the center of each strip.
Heat the oil in a deep fryer to 325°F (180°C). Cook in batches of two or three for 3 minutes each, turning the cookies over halfway through the cooking time. Drain on absorbent paper and sprinkle with sugar.

Pears in Red Wine

SERVES 4

INGREDIENTS: 4 large pears, peeled, quartered and cored - 1 bottle red wine - 1 cup (250 ml) raspberry liqueur (*crème de framboise*) - 1 orange - 2 cinnamon sticks - Scant 1 oz (25 g) superfine sugar - 1 bay leaf

Heat the wine in a saucepan. Add the raspberry liqueur. Cut the orange into thick slices crosswise, peel them, and add to the pan with the cinnamon sticks, superfine sugar, and bay leaf. Simmer for 10 minutes (without allowing the liquid to come to a full boil), then add the peeled pears.
Bring to the boil and simmer for 30 minutes. Leave to cool, then refrigerate. Serve cold.

DELIGHTS OF THE DAY

WHOLEGRAIN MUESLI

This is the European equivalent of granola, but not as crunchy.

SERVES 4

INGREDIENTS: 1^1/$_4$ oz (35 g) barley flakes - 1^1/$_4$ oz (35 g) buckwheat flakes - 1^1/$_4$ oz (35 g) raw oatmeal - 1–2 tbs light brown or dark brown sugar - 2 tsp (10 g) raisins - 4 dried apricots - 2 figs - 3 dates - 1 apple - 1 banana - 4 hazelnuts - 4 toasted almonds

The grains should preferably be organic. Combine them and sprinkle with the sugar (you can replace the sugar with dried fruit, using a heaped tablespoon of any or all of the following: dark or yellow raisins, dried apricots, dried figs, dates). Use a cheese grater to grate the apple and, to make a more nutritious mixture, add a banana cut into rounds. Finish with the hazelnuts and toasted almonds. Add whole milk or semi-skimmed milk, or use soy milk for a more easily digested dish.

NB: The fruits may vary depending on the season, but in the mountains muesli is often made with berries, such as strawberries, raspberries, and blueberries.

CHRISTMAS HOT CHOCOLATE

SERVES 4

INGREDIENTS: 14 oz (400 g) semi-sweet chocolate - ^{2}/$_3$ cup (150 g) granulated sugar - 2 cups (500 ml) light cream - 3 cups (750 ml) milk - 2 or 3 cinnamon sticks

Heat the sugar and light cream on medium heat, stirring constantly with a wooden spatula until a caramel forms.

Melt the chocolate over a low heat in a double boiler or bain-marie. Incorporate the chocolate into the caramel. Remove from the heat and leave to cool. The mixture can be kept for several hours in the refrigerator.

Boil the milk with the cinnamon sticks. Add the chocolate and caramel mixture to the cinnamon-flavored milk. Serve the chocolate in mugs or tall glasses, topped with a swirl of whipped cream.

TARENTAIS CAKE

INGREDIENTS: 8 large eggs - 1 cup (250 g) superfine sugar - 2 cups (500 g) butter - 3^1/$_2$ cups (500 g) ground almonds - 7 oz (200 g) honey - ^{2}/$_3$ cup (100 g) all-purpose flour - 3^1/$_2$ tbs (50 g) cornstarch

Preheat the oven to 275°F (140°C).

Use an electric beater to beat the eggs and sugar until thick and pale then gradually beat in the other ingredients. Bake for 2 hours in a *gugelhupf* mold, *bundt* pan, or angel food pan.

RUM CAKE

INGREDIENTS: ^{2}/$_3$ cup (150 g) softened butter - ^{2}/$_3$ cup (150 g) sugar - 4 eggs - 1^3/$_4$ cups (225 g) all-purpose flour - 1 tsp (6 g) baking powder - ^{1}/$_2$ cup (120 ml) rum

Preheat the oven to 425°F (220°C). Sift the flour and baking powder together.

Combine the butter and sugar until smooth and pale. Add the eggs one by one, then the rum. Incorporate the sifted flour. Butter and flour a deep cake pan, add the cake batter, and bake for approximately 10–15 minutes until the cake starts to color. Reduce the heat to 325°F (160°C) and bake for a further 45 minutes or until golden.

FLORENTINES

MAKES ABOUT 12

INGREDIENTS: 1^3/$_4$ oz (50 g) whole blanched almonds - 1^3/$_4$ oz (50 g) skinned hazelnuts - 1^3/$_4$ oz (50 g) whole pistachio nuts - 1^3/$_4$ oz (50 g) candied oranges - 10^1/$_2$ oz (300 g) semi-sweet baking chocolate

Preheat the oven to 325°F (180°C). Cover a greased cookie sheet with the nuts. Bake for 3 minutes. Leave to cool. Dice the candied oranges and add them to the cookie sheet. Melt the chocolate in a double boiler or bain-marie. Spread it over a sheet of nonstick baking paper slightly larger than the cookie sheet, leaving a 1-inch (2.5-cm) border. Then place the paper over the fruit and nuts, ensuring they stick to the chocolate. Leave in a cool place. Turn the sheet over and break the candy into pieces.

Provence

BETWEEN THE VINES, FLOWERS, AND AROMATIC HERBS,
THE MAGIC OF PROVENCE IS LIVED IN RHYTHM WITH THE SEASONS.
NATURE, EVER-PRESENT, DICTATES THE INFINITE NUANCES
OF A COLORFUL BUT NOT FOLKSY PALETTE, AND LENDS A HAND
IN THE DECORATION, INSIDE AND OUT.

A HOUSE
IN THE COUNTRY

The village of Ménerbes perches on a cliff above a sheer drop in a timeless setting. Lower down, somewhere on the road to Bonnieux, nestles La Bastide de Marie, where one would be well advised to make oneself known. Behind the heavy iron grille that slowly shuts all by itself, a long, majestic avenue of wind-breaking cypress and olive trees, bordered by sweet-smelling tufts of lavender, invites one to venture farther. From this moment, time will flow differently. Sheltered among the estate's twenty hectares of vine, this solid construction lies discreetly with its outhouses on a plot of land protected from without by hundred-year-old trees, like unmoving sentinels.

This typical Provençal country house combines all the advantages of a farm with those of a holiday home. The gate standing out in the middle of the fields, the broad, shady avenue that runs up to the entrance porch, the terrace, woods, fountains, and sculptures are all powerful components that structure the environment. It is a world apart; nevertheless it teems with life. Bees gather nectar from the roses, an ant colony follows its chosen route, the sun toys with the leaves, making patterns in light and shade. One catches a breath of air, rustling, the rhythms of nature. Then, at the end of the road-way, the imposing yet tranquil *bastide* awaits, an island of serenity, a haven and a refuge.

The most impressive thing about Provence is the proportions of the dwellings that have at some time swelled into veritable hamlets around a courtyard: farmhouse ranges that seem to sprout walls. In former times, the birth of a child meant a lean-to was converted into a house and a family home would evolve. At this time, no one built a new dwelling next to the old: the existing one was enlarged, with due regard to the privacy of the occupants. Whole families lived in houses to which so many rooms had been added that they now stood back to back. By the same token, one did not offload old furniture, but repaired it or repainted it, adapting it to the new living conditions.

At Ménerbes, in all humility, Jocelyne Sibuet learnt about the fragrances and savors of Provence, and especially those generous and sensual colors in which she revels. Eschewing stereotypes and folklore, she decided to retain only the overall impression. Without apparent effort, she has managed to wed the delights of comfort to the ever-changing demands of well-being. Also perhaps because she knows how to put the charm back into everyday life, to infuse it with an innocence redolent

The noble eighteenth-century *bastide* has been restored with the utmost respect for tradition and with the ease of day-to-day living in mind. The traditional iron and canvas deckchairs extend an open invitation to relax by the herb garden. A young vine grows along the farmhouse door, an entrance that has been painstakingly restored down to the last detail.

of the transitory world of childhood. If I had a house in Provence, one of her guests wrote one day, I would like it to be exactly like this one. Another lauded its "aggressively welcoming" atmosphere.

She did not know much about the land of Provence, however, before being beguiled more than five years ago by an eighteenth-century country house in a sorry state of repair standing in the very heart of the Lubéron Regional Nature Park. It had more than enough to satisfy the most insatiable lover of rickety stonework…. What is more, her adopted land is not only brimful of energy; it also possesses a unique magnetism. There, one feeds off the sun and the light, off sparks of joy, off the sonorous accents, the dizzying wind, and the numbing chant of the cicadas. Here, nature dictates a palette of countless shades that reflect seasonal rhythms. Here there are vines, trees, plants, flowers, aromatic herbs … a trained eye drinks in the infinite variations. One shouldn't forget either the impetuous mistral that sweeps all before it, whistling into sensitive ears and making everyone shiver, despite the blazing sun. And one also has to take into account the captivating fragrances released with such abandon by the lemon and fig trees, among others, which lean here and there against the tumbledown buttresses.

For a house is also part of the life which ebbs and flows around it, in step with time. Too much haste is likely to create mistakes: every location possesses a coherence that deserves to be attended to, to be felt, domesticated, understood. "One has to analyze what is already in situ, to deconstruct, then reconstruct it. To find what holds each story together. To take time to converse with the space as one explores it, approaching it like a living being and absorbing its logic."

In the end then, in this freestone manor house that she had originally intended to restore for her own family but which ended up being far too big, Jocelyne Sibuet installed fourteen private bedrooms. Proof, if proof were needed, that the magic of transmission only occurs when those who receive are able to appropriate their legacy completely, and to make it part of their own experience of life, of the world, and of their memory.

A sturdy enclave organically rooted to the ground, and virtually unaltered since it was built, with its walls and roof in a healthy state, the pile was of typical Provence construction, with substantial walls and narrow apertures as a defense against inclement weather, the mistral, and the sun. If in summer one often has the impression that Ménerbes is already in the south, winter can be as unkind here as in Megève! In the midst of its vineyards, yet lying wide open to the hills, the *bastide* is like an observatory in which one can detect nature's every breath, shiver, and sigh. In keeping with the harsh climate, the austere façade is richly adorned by a frame of ancient materials. Of perfect proportions, the lintel in old timber or polished stone hangs above the main door and serves to underline the nobility of the house.

The large portrait of unknown origin—stumbled across in a local bric-a-brac store—occupies the main wall in the drawing room. The traditional Provençal ceiling has been cleaned and carefully preserved, as have the beams. The natural harmonies of the walls are set off with a hint of khaki verging on beige; the color mauve dominates the sofas, armchairs, and curtains. The Baroque sconces and stool counterbalance the table's serious demeanor with patinated iron. The rusticity of the very fine and typically Provençal straw chair contrasts with the elegance of the gilt-wood couch.

The centerpiece, the immense old stone fireplace, serves, with its soothing mineral tones, as a rallying point for the whole family. Baroque couch, bookshelves, side table, chest of drawers, *chaise-lounge* … (preceding double page). The original colors of the antiques have been scrupulously preserved. The gilt-wood armchairs hold their own with more "relaxed" textiles. Here it is linen drape, though it might be denim upholstering a Louis XVI style and adding zip to the non-color of the honey and gingerbread color scheme. The top of the coffee table has been reworked with zinc to offer a more striking contrast (facing page, left). In a land where objects are used in all sorts of ways, everything is permitted. The lamp made out of a candlestick is of Italian origin, its shade underscoring the nuances of the room. Equally remarkable are the round oxblood chairs. The stone bust sets off the plain marble on a little table also found in Italy. An old skillet turned into a lamp is placed on the iron garden side table. The faded colors of the bookcase harmonize with the taupe-brown of the lampshade (left). The seasoned look of the recycled furniture is carefully preserved so as to lose nothing of that lived-in feel. Gilt-wood and tortoiseshell side table, glass knobs on the chest of drawers, and objets in twos—as here with the vases and prints—create a naive yet sophisticated blend (right).

Picked up in a market, the stone bust plays tone on tone with the exposed stone wall. Mixing different styles, even those which, on the face of it, have little in common, helps to unbutton the sometimes over-sophisticated look of period furniture. The coffee table is now used to display books and knick-knacks.

At first glance, the pure lines of the masonry conjured up a superb living space extending over several floors. In the years following its initial purchase, an eighteenth-century farmstead and a still-active *mas* (farmhouse) in the vicinity were absorbed into the estate and found their place in the family conversion. Thus the *bastide* could undergo its seamless transformation from stopover into convivial space.

The first stage of refurbishment concerned the main range, for which the interior circulation plan was redrawn, and several "bedroom/bathroom" modules devised. The exposed stone arches already bestowed a certain nobility on the decor; the weathered dry-stone walls were preserved, the ceilings raised in the traditional style, and the floors treated accordingly. Everywhere, Ménerbes or Oppède stone is used in the rough, the most natural possible to ensure unity of tone. The flagstones still bear visible marks of the passing of the years. Used from walls to flooring, the marble stone betrays within it—in the form of canals and slicks of color—the burden of its geological existence. Other stone includes recycled ashlar, exposed quoins, stone vaulting in the bedrooms. As it ages, the matt stone seems everlasting. Resistant and easy to maintain, it changes appearance depending on the treatment it undergoes, polishing or aging. Of various provenances and hewn from different blocks, each flagstone is practically unique.

The Ménerbes stone, used throughout
for flooring, is left rough. The staircase is
of uniform color, the banister rail all iron
simplicity, and the bookshelves, made to
measure by the master of the house,
have been patinated to the same soft
hue, creating a tranquil atmosphere
enhanced by the relaxed lines of the
occasional table and its accessories.
An earthenware jar has been spirited
from the outside to the inside.

On the floor are terracotta tiles once again, *mallons* once applied to the ceiling and now employed for a different use. When thinking about how to make the most of an interior space, the first priority is to pinpoint the elements of sensory and aesthetic comfort one wishes to obtain. Well-being, then, and visual satisfaction. At the outset, the light-colored flooring, the stone walls, the linen bedcovers, and the sofas covered in plain fabric are keynotes in an approach that, luminous and airy, reinforces the generosity and simplicity of the locale.

The main living space occupies the volume of the barn that was preserved intact. The old oak beams were exposed to the light of day and the walls lime-washed in subtle colors. The natural harmonies are brought out with a hint of khaki verging on beige for the walls, and a predominantly mauve monochrome on the settees and armchairs. Here too, that focus of family life, the immense fireplace hewn out of the solid stone, reappears. The gilded-wood Louis XVI-style armchairs are curiously upholstered in denim to chivy up the want of ambient color. It may well be fitting to keep faith with Provençal traditions, but this does not mean lapsing into cliché.

The watchwords, then, are: space, light, color. "I based the space on the delicate hues I could see around me. In the vineyards, on the plain, and in the hills hereabouts. I started out with the plants of Provence, the bright pastels one finds throughout the region, and with the highly individual beige of the area's stone." And then she took note of the mistral that sweeps the path, whistles in the ears, and has one shivering behind the sun. She listened to the rhythm of time and to the gentle lessons of things. She hearkened to life around her, pacing herself, avoiding over-hasty interpretations. Only then was she to begin refurbishing the *bastide* and its outbuildings, guided by her sensations and steering clear of the obvious. At La Bastide de Marie, every detail is dictated by nature. It is from her influence that such abundance—all this pleasure for the eyes—is born. As the seasons turn, the plants set the tone for the color schemes in the house.

In adapting the interior space, Jocelyne has gone for a sensory, emotional, aesthetic comfort. For her, this is one of life's golden rules. One might even say that what she bestowed on the smoothness of the Ménerbes stone was what it lacked: furniture that seemed lived in, objects or old squares of mortar picked up secondhand or from antique dealers. She combed auction rooms, where decisions have to be taken early and quickly. "The best deals are clinched in the first half hour. I only buy on the spur of the moment." Found or salvaged, these articles represent values, a history perhaps, a point of reference certainly. They encapsulate a timeless past, the deep sheen of time. "I proceed by coincidences," the mistress of the house says, acknowledging her deep-rooted attachment to the values of childhood and family. Her rules, however, are her own.

This room has been dubbed "ivory white," because of its monochrome color scheme, ranging from purest white to khaki and putty in bleached gradations. So as not to shock the eye, no one note is higher than the other, with the same harmonies running from bedroom to boudoir and right through to the bathroom. Even the stone has been repainted, emphasizing the sober majesty of a duo of eighteenth-century cabriolet armchairs. A gossamer curtain or a hanging that allows in the light or billows in the wind blurs the frontier between exterior and interior.

In the kitchen, the open shelving leaves all the utensils within easy reach. Activity is centered around the main piece of furniture in the room, the butcher's table. Faux marble protects the wall around the fine old sink. The pantry has been treated in nuances of gray and marbling, providing it with a well-earned lift. Against the four green doors of an old wood dresser, the transparent glass basins and cloches offer a contrast to the superior pout of an Arlésienne in her Sunday best.

Initially, she buys the larger pieces—bookshelves, sofas, a big armchair, for example—before adding the movable elements in the decoration and the accessories. An initial burst of enthusiasm, and the rest of the story follows accordingly. The key is to remain coherent, and in particular to respect the original spaces. Jocelyne offers her objects houseroom, juxtaposing them, arranging and gathering them so they can begin a new existence. For everything has a place, its own place—here today, there tomorrow. The weathered look that she likes to preserve—everything is restored in an authentic manner using traditional materials and techniques—gives the impression they have always belonged within these four walls. This amounts almost to her trademark. There is not a single piece that does not have a very personal story to tell. And, whatever she appropriates, whenever she has recourse to an object that comes freighted with a collective memory, this shared nostalgia confers still greater emotional impact.

"Often, I place objects side by side, playing with even numbers, with the pair. The resulting symmetry is especially rewarding." On the walls she sticks prints and drawings. "I work with the material of a drawing to provide a light, expressive touch."

The kitchen ceiling has been brushed to keep that lived-in, time-worn look. The large cornice is dressed with faux marble to counterbalance the hood. The stone double sink, the old stove, the bistro table, and the cupboard—all picked up in local antique shops—impart a feeling of *déjà-vu* in an original-style kitchen that is fitted with the most up-to-date technical equipment available.

She cannot conceive of a living space without old books, without great bookcases from which you can grab something that catches your eye as you walk past. "The [shelves] contain treasures, forgotten anthologies, works that at one time somebody probably loved. Beyond their functional, practical utility, they paint an immaterial landscape, a heaven-sent springboard for the imagination."

Luminosity and sunshine remain essential qualities in any dwelling. It is critical when restoring a house in Provence to leave the doors and windows as they are, copying the slopes of the original roof. The buildings of the ancients demonstrate a respect for natural cycles and take the vagaries of the climate into consideration. They knew its every trick. The stifling heat of a Provençal summer can be followed by a winter that is equally rigorous. The windows are calculated with this in mind, deliberately narrow to keep the cold as well as the heat at bay. The arrow-slits with fixed panes let in little of the sun's rays. Similarly, the relieves round the windows are beveled to filter out the light, making a gap in which foods that need to be kept cool can be stored.

Light has a purpose, but it is also a source of beauty. However, if one is not careful, it will flood in unconstrained. Pouring in through the lofty windows, it reverberates on the glistening stone slabs, tempered only by the great wooden shutters that are essential for keeping out the blazing heat and regulating the shade. The custom in Provence is to keep them tight shut during the hottest hours of the day, throwing them wide open come evening to allow cooler air to waft into the house.

In short, the art consists in knowing how to master light, to control it, to filter it. And to turn it to good effect. The window is not the only element through which one can play with light: materials, colors, and furniture are just as important. Wooden floors react to light quite differently from metal surfaces; it soon becomes clear that the sun is the ideal way to bring out colors. One way to do this is by opting for white walls, for example, which reflect sunbeams and moderate their intensity at various hours of the day. Specialists have long been amazed at the mysterious connections between color and light. Technically speaking, a white surface reflects the totality (or the near totality) of the light. When evening falls, daylight—which can be soft and diffuse—is extended in the *bastide* and its outbuildings by way of artificial but indirect illumination. "I prefer tall standard lamps that provide good light in the rooms, and mirrors to reflect and give a softer focus to the environment. I like to draw people to the window to direct them to what deserves to be seen: the landscape, nature...."

The subtlety of lighting presently available on the market makes it possible to install a broad range of lighting fitments. Warm or chilly, electric light can be modulated at will, lighting an entire room or spotlighting a table. Today, moreover, light sources are increasingly unobtrusive, and can be concealed, leaving only portable lamps in view.

A Baroque environment dominated by grays stands beneath a chandelier with Venetian accents that contrasts with the stone flooring in monochrome checkerboard. The gilded-wood console gives a sophisticated twist to a wall that has retained its old face. On the table, braided in matching tones, the bouquets remind one of the countryside outside. Whether composed of branches and dry leaves, or of flowers freshly cut from the garden, or of artichokes and heather, as here, they are never domineering; they melt into the ambient harmony. Candles, bracket lights, and a chandelier provide the perfect lighting scheme.

BEDROOMS
IN NATURAL COLORS

The high ceilings in the bedrooms of the *bastide* further entertain this sense of majesty and well-being: the spaces, the building materials selected, the quality of the natural light, the choice of the furniture, accessories, and fabrics, complete the ambience.

"Before being anything else, I am a colorist. Color summons up a feeling of life, of energy. I like to observe. In the first place, Provence brings with it a color scheme unlike anything I ever see in the mountains. It displays another chromatic palette, a gamut of countless unusual and sometimes austere nuances derived from the seasons, a panoply of tones that don't really have the time to settle down at higher altitudes. I feel the need to integrate nature into daily life. I am very sensitive to subtle harmonies of brown—for example, on leaves, flowers, and plants when the season suddenly shifts. I love it when I can see that trace of dust, of powder, of time forgotten. In conjunction with more colorful flowers, these plants act like developing fluid, a perfect ground that tends to the somber, yet which underscores the luminous quality of the whole. The ever-changing reflections of vine leaves—sanguine and golden—are also a rich source of inspiration. Inexhaustible. Shakespeare wrote that art, in itself, is nature. That is the only model. Just like the soft pastels in the square plot of herbs. I have a particular tenderness for the gentle notes of aromatic herbs: gray, green, sage colored; a pretty trio that I take up in my interiors in continuity with the basic exterior harmonies. Thus, on the *bastide* walls, I mixed khaki with chestnut-brown and beige to contrast with the non-color of the Ménerbes stone that was laid on all the floors and which we wanted to conserve as pure, as rugged as possible. When one is self-taught, like me, one has to mix things up, try them out, throw them around. Things do not always turn out right first time. But that's no problem; one just starts over, ready to try out more combinations. Now, I carry out trials. I have always enjoyed doing things in opposing colors and materials."

Warm tones are a stimulant; cool tones have a assuaging influence. Green floats somewhere between the two, a mediator in the dispute. Yellow brings dynamism, cheerfulness, red plenitude and exuberance, and blue its mystery. This is the color scheme that reappears in Provençal prints, in skirts and petticoats from Arles that long ago were cut from the most sophisticated materials, such as dyed silk.

Embarking on her preparatory research in the rooms of the Museum at Arles, Jocelyne fell in love with the work of a local nineteenth-century painter, Léo Lelée. And, more than all the others, one picture by this artist, the *Farandole des Arlésiennes*,

The little serving table, flowery and adorned with a candle, sets off the cordial simplicity and precision of a decor that is all tranquil harmony. The bookcase for example, has been preserved "as it came" and soberly restored. The most important things are the books it contains.

Fresh and transparent linen gauze is draped over the clean-cut lines of an iron baldachin (facing page). Here and there, some *boutis* fabric has been delicately laid. To add to the interest of the chair, the linen cushion has been stuffed and upholstered. Natural light brings out the airiness of the sunny cottons. The head of the bed (right) is a two-tone affair, and the traditional woods have been stained dark to match. The focus is on opposites: though dark gray dominates, its various tonalities coincide harmoniously.

marked her profoundly. It inspired a decor in one of the *bastide*'s suites in various shades of red. "I wanted the curtains to remind one not only of bridal skirts, but also of the dresses worn by girls in Arles. They were fitted with an underskirt that adds volume and an elegant, sophisticated flounce." And, of course, a lithograph reproducing this famous picture adorns the bedroom. Permeated by Southern French joviality, it is balanced by a refined, delicate, precious white, whose subtlety is enhanced by the understated palette. Subdued hints of brighter notes appear—a madder-colored armchair here, bright red silk under curtains there. Just touches, though, nothing more. She never over-does it, and prefers a fine linen or a calico embroidered by Edith Mézard, her neighbor in Goult, to other, somewhat gaudier cotton fabrics. Jocelyne also harks back to the spirit of old *boutis* fabrics, reinterpreting, updating them. And in the large drawing room, the immense Baroque couch is covered in blue denim, thereby bringing out the Cretan urns and the worn marble. Naturally, it is a denim that is manufactured locally.

Here and there, she'll set a leaf or two, as if to show up their astonishing patterns. They enfold within them all the magic and wild beauty of the plant world. Elsewhere, leaves accompany a jumble of stone ornaments roped in from the garden,

PRECEDING DOUBLE PAGE:
Eiderdowns and blankets pile up. Traditional Provence *boutis* are mixed with satin piqué, velvets, and linens. The toile de Jouy-style headboard, an early twentieth-century reproduction, is painted in the same tones and goes well with the antique wooden frame. The stress is laid on the freshness, transparency, and lightness of the bed canopy.

LEFT:
The parallel beams of the Provençal ceiling counter the fretwork rococo of a secondhand headboard with central monogram. The corner piece is built out of some old doors.

FACING PAGE:
The small bedside chair is in gilt wood. Each room bears the name of a plant from the garden. Reflected in the old mirror, one can appreciate the mysterious rapport between color and light. An iron canopy and *boutis*, tapestry cushions and period *cabriolet*—that's all it takes to create an atmosphere. A cleverly orchestrated accumulation of objects and accessories; of books on shelves, or lying about, seemingly forgotten, on a chair; the flicker of a diminutive candle: all create a feeling of soothing intimacy.

Gris de Sauge

Continuing from the bedroom, the bathroom is always treated as a living space in its own right, in what is an individual reinterpretation of the boudoirs of yesteryear. A console table or an iron *gueridon* is slipped between the bathtubs. These are raised on feet with large rolled sides. The baths and hand basins are all modern reproductions of older models. Magic potions, a mint bouquet, jars with herb teas and tisanes, flasks of oil—so many invitations to treat yourself well. Around the bathtub, faux marble protects the wall; the mirror reflects it all. The ample linen curtain can be drawn across to separate bathroom from bedroom.

or night-lights and candles in rows on the long central table. Some are almost works of art in themselves, and Jocelyne will even go so far as to arrange them under a glass dish cover with three sprigs of lavender and a book selected from her bedside reading. In these parts, one appreciates the bedroom, especially during the precious hours of the siesta, when as each second passes, time slows down.

Since shared pleasures were uppermost in Jocelyne's mind as she began her designs, the essential difficulty lay in getting the individual and the group, the personal and the collective, to cohabit. This need for privacy, for finding a space of one's own, a territory, is something we all feel. Such sensory comforts must take into account the quality of the local light and sounds. And the bedroom, more than any other room, represents the secret garden: confidentiality. Anyone coming to this refuge wants to gain peace, to unwind, even to escape, symbolically. This explains again why nothing should be systematic, nothing should look like anything else. Each bedroom acquires its own personality based on a single color theme: lime-tree green, sage gray, aster mauve, blue jean, aniseed…. As we've said, everything is organized around nature's plants, even if this means indulging in some intense oppositions or resorting to the monochrome, according to whim or necessity.

More often than not, Jocelyne tends to leave bedrooms as they are: she likes to preserve their original spirit. Overdoing the finish, over-egging the pudding can kill the soul of a place in the process. "I prefer to keep that little defect that accentuates the personality. The plump curve, for example, of a swelling wall, peeling, damaged, is an imperfection that gives a narrow corridor a relief it would sorely miss were it 'made good' in the conventional manner. Or else those walls painted in two colors divided halfway up by a dado to add depth, something one used to see rather often in old houses. Neither am I averse to mixing styles that are in theory mutually exclusive, because I like to upset things that look oversophisticated. Gilded wood, of particular interest to me when it comes to giving new life to a secondhand chair, gains greatly in personality when combined with relaxed fabrics, such as denim or heavy hessian." An Arles merino blanket or a bolt of rough local linen could equally provide the stimulus for some inspirational decorating.

To know how to freshen things up is vital; in an ideal house, the bedroom opens directly onto a bathroom, which, even if it is rudimentary, can look luxurious. Or double up: a functional little shower box for a quick wash and a bathtub for a voluptuous soak. In any case, more than any other room, it is the place one should be able to forget the outside world and relax. Perhaps the height of luxury is quite simply a vast bathtub filled with hot water in which one can read, daydream, sing, or receive visitors.

In the *bastide*, the bathroom is treated as a fully fledged living area. As a place devoted to personal care, it deserves careful attention. Even if it is first and foremost a functional space dedicated to bodily hygiene, today it has become far more than somewhere to perform one's ablutions. It tends to become a place to be alone, a room from which one draws renewed strength. Some people put in a sofa and turn it into a sitting room. "If need be, I'll leave the bath in the middle of the room—or, better still, in front of the window so as to benefit from the view over nature."

THE ART OF
OUTDOOR LIVING

Life in the sun is lived to a different rhythm, another way of organizing time. One could almost divide one's day between in and out, between light and shade. The hours spent out on the terrace or in the garden are intimately linked to the way one lives in the house. So as to benefit from the cool air in the small hours, or to let in a breeze during the course of the day, there are doors and windows to slide, push, or throw open.

The patio and interior courtyard, the gently sloping terrace, serve as open-air reception rooms beneath a broad sky…. Besides, who has never dreamed of sleeping in the summer months under the stars in the shadow of a lime or plane tree?

The house is a space that moves, a private place that reconciles a need for security and a desire to remain open to the exterior. The patio and the inner courtyard are treated as extensions of the main room: one can easily not realize one has gone from inside to out—or vice versa. The breeze buoys you along; you drag out a table, then hang the hammock wherever the fancy takes you. In the *bastide*, objects pass almost indiscriminately from in to out, from house to garden, following the changing season, the variations of the sun. "Inside, I think it's nice to find a place for a plaster angel or two, for busts normally intended for the garden. Detaching them from their initial function gives them a fresh vitality."

At the front door of the house, there are several passports to escapism: chimes, and a cropped Italian curtain made of fishing line and boxwood balls that shifts in the wind. Their tinkling, as well as shooing away wasps and other insects, sounds an invitation to escape. Above all, it reverberates in the imagination. Both the chairs and the table are simple pieces of furniture made of iron or wood, easily transported from one corner of the great, trellis-shaded terrace to the other. Around the swimming pool, little mattresses add to the comfort of the wicker settee, the deckchairs and benches for three are a godsend for the lazy, while the plain cotton cushions and pillows can be scattered at will. Discreet but palpable, homemade pottery brings its own bright touch of local color. When, at nightfall,

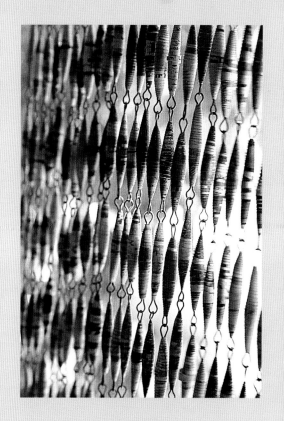

This spring-linen-covered iron deckchair, and the broad tarpaulin shading it, are a blatant invitation to laze about. Fragrances of the South surround the patio, which was designed as a natural prolongation of the house, a living space where one can hardly tell whether one's in or out. The transition is imperceptible and keeps the air fresh and cool. The muffled music of the wind rustles through the colorful bead curtain, marking the passing of time.

little candles burn on the terrace, fleeting odors waft through the air, and the sound of silence calms the world.

Eating outside is yet another daily ritual, enjoyed in the flowery shade of the arbor, or beneath a trellis, an olive tree, or even a veranda or covered yard. Here, as elsewhere, cooking is experienced as a way of better appreciating the wonders of nature. One has but to open one's eyes to feed the imagination, to give one's inspiration free rein.

At the *bastide*, whatever the hour, beneath the wisteria or the fig, a plate of delicacies awaits new arrivals. As befits the country, this is a friendly get-together, free of showy luxury—though the aperitif is a hallowed oasis of peace. Pastoral, covered in flowers, sober and simple, but a gourmet treat, nonetheless! You trot to

The unexpected hues of these tartan cushions coordinate with the natural brown tones of the table, which is laid in an unpretentious and relaxed manner for a spot of country lunch. On the console lie extras and accessories. A night-light, an oil bottle knotted with raffia—every detail is honed to perfection. The velvety feel of sage leaves and their subtle greenish-gray tone reappear around the house.

the long table, laid with white cotton, which stands in front of the vine. Your mood is set fair. Or you enjoy the luxury of taking lunch under the lime tree. For some, the lime is regarded as a spiritual bond between the underworld and the earthly realm. This is perhaps why, since the dawn of time, it has symbolized the spirit of conviviality and of communion: it often has pride of place in a festive scene.

From the Renaissance to the beginning of the twentieth century, the Provence garden was one laid out around a *bastide*. The one we are talking about now is fortunate enough to lie well protected in the Lubéron Regional Nature Park. The opulent colors of the vine adorn the estate—and there is nothing to add to that. One just has to know how to make the most of it. A handful of plants grace the foreground, so that the eye is drawn to the vineyards and the plain of the Lubéron beyond. A climate that can be severe necessarily limits extravagance: plants are selected primarily for their hardiness. Plane trees, boxwood groves, olive and lemon trees are the stalwarts, fond favorites. There are rare species in the herb garden too: pineapple sage with the sugary taste of the fruit, angelica, melissa that can be added to aniseed in a homemade herb tea that has more than one taker, the immortelle, the arquebus, and the hyssop.... A privileged hideaway through which wafts the balmy scent of freedom.

At the entrance to the house, a traditional curtain made of boxwood keeps the interior cool. The inner courtyard was recreated from scratch. Stone walls were created from the *restanques* (old retaining walls in the fields) and paved with recycled flagstones. The *calade* pebbling was made entirely by hand by a local craftsman in the traditional way. Honeysuckle and mulberry perfume the outer terrace, where a braided straw pouf with ecru cover, old chairs, and an iron coffee table welcome one at teatime or for an aperitif.

PAGES 108–109:

The swimming pool, comfortably appointed for those lazy days, is a meeting place for all. It shelters from the winds of Provence behind a wall built in chunky stone. The basin, into which the tap runs continuously, is treated in shades of green to echo the soft vegetal hues surrounding it. The roof over the small patio was built using old tiles, and the iron beds were designed in the spirit of the region. The curtains insulate a space in which it is glorious to relax with a cup of sage tea.

MARDI 2 Août

• Le Petit Artichaut Violet Mijoté
soit L'y Laisse poêlés au Thym.

• La Soupe de Tomates de la Bastide
Crème de Chèvre Frais, pain aux
olives.

• L'Aile de Raie dorée à la Marjolaine
Céleri Blanc aux Agrumes confits.

• Le Rôti de Veau de Lait en Broche,
Carottes et Échalotes glacées au
Romarin

Le Plateau de Fromages.

• Le Rouleau Craquant Framboises
pépin et sorbet aux fruits de la
passion

• L'Abricot Rôti au Caramel de
Provence, crème glacée à l'huile
d'olive Vierge.

Tomates Séchées
au Soleil

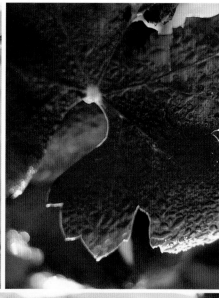

Country fragrances and savors are the order of the day at table. Today, there are sun-dried tomatoes and specialties from the South. Beneath the trees, which keep one cool and fresh, enjoy an aromatic tisane made with thyme, rosemary, and sage gathered from the herb garden nestling behind a low wall. Next to the imposing stone table, a rose tree gives off its natural bouquet. It's no chore to lay the table in the shade on the open terrace or, as in former times, under the lime tree, in front of the parti-colored vine. The long, narrow iron table recalls meals served during the grape harvest. The greenhouse and orangery have also been converted into ideal places for relaxation, but, by the end of the day, the family generally gathers for a glass or two in the garden.

Aperitifs

Open-faced Baby Vegetable Sandwiches

Serves 4

INGREDIENTS: 3 baby globe artichokes - 8 baby carrots - 2 tbs olive oil - 4 slices wholewheat bread - 5 tbs (80 g) pesto - 4 preserved tomatoes - 16 pitted black olives, sliced into rings

The day before, clean and trim the artichokes and cook in a pressure cooker. Then remove all the leaves, just keeping the hearts. Cut the hearts into 4 and marinate in the olive oil for 24 hours.

On the day, drain the artichokes. Fry for 10 to 15 minutes with the carrots then leave to cool, and refrigerate.

Heat the olive oil in a frying pan and sauté the slices of bread. Pat with kitchen paper to absorb any of the excess olive oil.

Spread the slices of bread with the pesto. Add the artichokes, preserved tomatoes, the carrots, and the olives.

Yellow and Red Tomato Terrine with Basil and Goat Milk Yogurt

Serves 8

INGREDIENTS: 9lb (4 kg) of red tomatoes - 9lb (4 kg) of yellow tomatoes - 2 tablespoons olive oil - Salt and pepper - 1 garlic clove, crushed - 1 bunch of thyme - Granulated sugar - 2 tbs unflavored gelatin softened in 4 tsp water, or according to manufacturer's instructions - 2 cups (500 ml) tomato juice - 2 tbs ketchup - 1 tbs tomato paste - 3 drops Tabasco - 2$\frac{1}{4}$ lb (1 kg) fresh basil - 1 cup (250 g) very fresh goat cheese

Preheat the oven to 200°F (110°C).

Slice the tomatoes into rounds about $\frac{1}{8}$ in (3 mm) thick. Arrange them on a cookie sheet, overlapping them slightly, but without mixing the reds and yellows. Brush them with olive oil, then sprinkle with salt, pepper, crushed garlic, and fresh thyme. Finish with a pinch of sugar to reduce the acidity of the tomatoes. Place in the oven to dry out for 1 hour.

Soften the gelatin in 4 tablespoons water or follow the manufacturer's instructions. Bring the tomato juice to the boil with the ketchup and tomato paste. Then add salt, pepper, Tabasco, and a pinch of sugar. Stir in the softened gelatin. Leave the tomato aspic in the refrigerator for a few moments to cool, but do not let it set.

When the tomatoes are cooked, remove the cookie sheet from the oven. Line a terrine with plastic wrap leaving a generous overhanging edge that can be wrapped over the top of the terrine.

Pour a small ladleful of the (still liquid) aspic into the terrine, then arrange the yellow tomatoes on top. Add a layer of basil leaves, then a layer of red tomatoes and continue layering until the terrine is full. Wrap the plastic wrap over the top and pierce it with a few holes. Press down on it using another mold of the same shape so that the excess aspic runs out. Refrigerate for at least 6 hours.

To serve, slice the terrine thinly. Dice the fresh goat cheese and scatter around the terrine. Sprinkle with a little olive oil. Serve immediately.

Toasts with Sheep's Milk Cheese and Goat Cheese

Serves 4

INGREDIENTS: 4 slices of country bread - olive oil - 6 tbs (80 g) *caillé de brebis* (sheep's milk) cheese - 3 tbs (40 g) dry, aged goat cheese - 4 sprigs chive - 8 leaves wild rocket

Toast the slices of country bread, and sprinkle with a few drops of olive oil. Spread the *caillé de brebis* cheese over the toasts. Cut a few slices of the goat cheese and place them across the toasts. Decorate with the chives and wild rocket.

LUNCHEON UNDER THE LIME TREE

BASTIDE TOMATO SOUP WITH OLIVE OIL AND CHOPPED PISTACHIOS

SERVES 8
INGREDIENTS: 9 lb (4 kg) very ripe tomatoes - 3 cups (750 ml) tomato juice - 8 tbs ketchup - 4 tsp tomato paste - 1 tsp ground fennel - 1 tsp ground aniseed - 1 tsp powdered tomato - $^1/_2$ teaspoon chopped garlic - Salt and freshly ground black pepper - 4 tbs (80 g) toasted pistachios, coarsely chopped - $^2/_5$ cup (100 ml) extra-virgin olive oil

Wash the tomatoes and cut them into eight slices. Combine all the ingredients except the olive oil. Blend and strain through a conical sieve. Add the olive oil, whisking well. Season with salt and pepper.
Serve sprinkled with the chopped pistachios.

BROILED EGGPLANT

SERVES 4
INGREDIENTS: 3 medium eggplants - 1 cup (250 ml) olive oil - 1 sprig thyme - 2 bay leaves - 1 sprig rosemary - 1 garlic clove - 10 currants or other fresh berries

Slice the eggplants and blanch them quickly in boiling water.
Dip the eggplant slices in the olive oil.
Broil them in a frying pan until cooked.
Leave the eggplant to marinate for 48 hours in a pot with the olive, herbs, and flavorings.
Drain the eggplant before serving.

GOAT CHEESE MARINADE

TO MAKE 1 POT
INGREDIENTS: 1 garlic clove - 1 sprig of thyme - 1 bay leaf - 1 sprig of rosemary - Ecus de Babette and Catherine goat cheese - Olive oil

Put the garlic, thyme, bay leaf, and rosemary into a jar. Cut the cheese in half and add to the jar. Cover with olive oil and leave to marinate for 1 week.

BASTIDE HERB TEA

TO MAKE 1 QUART (1 LITER) HERB TEA
INGREDIENTS: 2 tbs lemon verbena - 1 tbs thyme - 1 lemon
Put the herbs in a teapot and cover with 1 quart (1 liter) lightly boiling water. Leave to infuse. Serve with two or three lemon slices.

LUNCH UNDER THE LIME TREE

SUN-DRIED TOMATOES ON THE VINE

SERVES 8

INGREDIENTS: 9 lb (4 kg) tomatoes on the vine - Extra-virgin olive oil - Salt and freshly ground black pepper - Sugar - 4 garlic cloves, peeled and sliced - 10 sprigs of thyme (wild if possible) - 2 bay leaves - 2 rosemary sprigs

Clean the tomatoes and dry the skins well; discard the stalk. Slice them into 6 or 8 rounds, depending on their size.

Sprinkle a cookie sheet with a little olive oil, a little salt, sugar and freshly ground black pepper. Arrange the tomatoes on the sheet close together, and sprinkle them with salt, sugar, and freshly ground black pepper. Add the sliced garlic cloves and sprinkle with thyme.

Cook in an oven preheated to 200°F (100°C) for 2 hours, sprinkling with olive oil every 45 minutes.

Transfer the tomatoes to a $10^{1}/_{2}$ oz (300 g) glass jar with the thyme, bay leaf, and rosemary, and cover with the olive oil. Leave to marinate for at least 5 days.

Drain on absorbent paper before serving.

Serve as a condiment or to accompany a salad.

In Provence in the summer, tomatoes are sundried for 12 hours.

RED PLUM TART

SERVES 6–8

INGREDIENTS: 5 lb (2 kg) red plums - 1 tbs (15 g) butter - 1 tbs superfine sugar

SHORTCRUST DOUGH:

$^{2}/_{3}$ cup (150 g) softened butter - 1 tsp granulated sugar - 2 cups (250 g) all-purpose flour - 1 egg - 5 tablespoons (60 ml) milk - 1 pinch of salt

FILLING:

$6^{1}/_{4}$ tbs (90 g) brown sugar - $6^{1}/_{4}$ tbs (90 g) ground almonds - $^{1}/_{3}$ cup (100 g) egg whites - 9 tbs (120 g) butter - $2^{1}/_{2}$ tbs (30 g) all-purpose flour

Combine all the ingredients for the shortcrust dough using an electric mixer on low speed, and finish by hand to roll the dough into a ball. Wrap it in plastic wrap and refrigerate for 3 hours. Roll out chilled dough and use it to line a tart pan. Return it to the refrigerator to rest for 30 minutes.

To prepare the filling, combine the brown sugar and ground almonds. Add the egg whites and the butter cut into lumps. Finish by incorporating the sifted all-purpose flour. Pour this mixture into the tart and chill in the refrigerator.

Heat the oven to 350°F (175°C).

Cut the plums three-quarters of the way through lengthwise so as to be able to remove the pit while keeping the fruit whole.

Melt 1 tbs (15 g) butter.

Arrange the plums on the tart. Sprinkle with the melted butter and then with the sugar.

Bake for at least 15 minutes or until the pastry is golden.

Harvest Menu

Terrine of Dressed Leeks and Chicken Liver Mousse

Serves 6

Ingredients: 6 lb 8 oz (3 kg) medium leeks - 1 quart (1 liter) veal or chicken stock - Grainy French mustard - Salt and pepper - 4 tbs unflavored gelatin - 2¼ lb (1 kg) chicken livers - Butter for frying - 2 tbs (10 ml) cognac - 3 cups (750 ml) light cream - Canola oil - Old wine vinegar - 1 loaf wholewheat bread - Chervil leaves

Prepare the terrine the night before serving. Separate the whole white parts and green parts of the leeks. Steam the white parts and blanch the green parts. Drain. Heat the stock, add the mustard, salt and pepper and the gelatin. Line a rectangular terrine with the green parts of the leeks. Add the white parts of the leeks to the terrine. Pour the mixture of stock, gelatin, and mustard over the white parts until it reaches the top of the terrine. Leave in a cool place to set. Sauté the chicken livers in a little butter, then flambé in the cognac and leave to cool. Grind them in a food processor and push through a sieve. Beat with the light cream to obtain a mousse. Make the dressing by combining the canola oil, wine vinegar, and mustard. Toast the wholewheat bread.
Slice the terrine and arrange it on a plate with a spoonful of liver mousse, a half slice of bread, the dressing, and the chervil leaves.

Apple Dumplings

Serves 4

Ingredients: 4 firm, tart apples - 2½ oz (100 g) puff dough - 2 egg whites - 2 tbs (50 g) superfine sugar

Preheat the oven 325°F (170°C).
Wrap each apple in puff dough.
Use a pastry brush to coat each dumpling in egg white.
Sprinkle with the sugar.
Bake for 30 minutes.

Provençal Beef Stew with Yellow Chanterelles and Broiled Waxy Potatoes

Serves 4
Ingredients:

For the stew: 3lb 5 oz (1.5 kg) lean cubed stewing beef - 1 onion - 2 carrots - 1 leek - 1 celery stalk - 2 tomatoes - 2 bottles of Domaine de Marie red wine- 1 sprig of thyme - 1 sprig of rosemary - 1 bay leaf - 10 juniper berries - 2 garlic cloves

Garnish: 1 lb 2 oz (500 g) small, waxy potatoes - 1½ cups (300 g) yellow chanterelles (wild mushrooms) - 1 shallot - 1 sprig flat-leaved parsley - 1 pinch salt - 1 pinch pepper - 3 tbs (50 g) butter

Wash the stew vegetables and cut them into small pieces.
Marinate the meat, stew vegetables, and all the flavorings in the wine overnight. Put them in a cast-iron pot with a lid and simmer for four hours. Meanwhile, clean the potatoes thoroughly without peeling. Broil then add to the stew pot about two and a half hours after the start of cooking time. Clean and slice the chanterelles. Sauté them in a frying pan with the chopped shallot.
When the stew is cooked, remove the meat and potatoes and reserve. Strain the cooking liquid into another pot and discard all the vegetables. Reduce the cooking liquid by half, gradually beating in the butter. Return the meat and the potatoes to the pot, adding the chanterelles. Sprinkle with the finely-chopped parsley. Serve hot.

Dinner for Two

Provençal Meatballs in Vine Leaves

SERVES 2

INGREDIENTS: 1 oz (25 g) soft breadcrumbs - Milk - 4 vine leaves - Wine vinegar - 12 black grapes - $^1/_2$ lb (250 g) pigeon meat - $1^1/_2$ oz (40 g) pig's liver or chicken livers - 1 bunch flat-leaved parsley - 1 bunch chives - $^1/_4$ oz (8 g) shallots - 1 garlic clove - 1 pinch of salt - 1 pinch of pepper - 1 tsp of ground mixed spice - 1 cup (160 ml) meat *jus* - 1 tbs butter - 1 tbs olive oil - A few strands of raffia to truss the meatballs

Soak the breadcrumbs in a little milk.
Soak the vine leaves in water with a little vinegar.
Slice the grapes in half, discarding the seeds.
Grind the meats with the drained breadcrumbs, herbs, and spices, and add the grapes. Shape into 4 identically sized balls. Lay each on a drained vine leaf and tie up with the raffia.
Place the balls in a Dutch oven or casserole, add the meat *jus*, cover, and simmer on a low heat for 20 minutes, basting them from time to time.
When cooked, take the meatballs out of the pot and keep them warm while reducing the gravy.
Add the butter and olive oil to the gravy and blend in a food processor. Serve the meatballs coated in the sauce.

Warm Vegetable Salad

SERVES 2

INGREDIENTS: $1^3/_4$ oz (50 g) carrots - $1^3/_4$ oz (50 g) turnips - $1^3/_4$ oz (50 g) green beans - $1^3/_4$ oz (50 g) leeks - $1^3/_4$ oz (50 g) baby green beans - $1^3/_4$ oz (50 g) zucchini - $1^3/_4$ oz (50 g) tomatoes - Chervil - Basil - Mint - Chives - Dill

DRESSING:

$^1/_2$ cup (125 ml) dandelion honey (see stockist, below) - $^1/_3$ cup (100 ml) dandelion liqueur (see stockist, below) - $1^1/_4$ cups (300 ml) old wine vinegar - $1^1/_4$ cups (300 ml) canola oil

Steam the vegetables.
Heat the honey until it caramelizes, then moisten it with the liqueur and wine vinegar.
Add the canola oil.
Combine the herbs with the vegetables and sprinkle with the dressing.
Serve warm.

The dandelion honey and liqueur can be bought from Oh! Legumes oubliés, Château de Belloc, 33 670 Sadirac. Tel.: 05 56 30 61 00 www.ohlegumesoublies.com

Dinner for Two

Baked Figs with Bay Leaves

Serves 2

Ingredients:

6 figs
6 bay leaves
1 tbs (15 g) sugar
6 toothpicks

Reduction:

1/2 cup (125 ml) fresh ripe
  peach juice
1 bay leaf
2 tsp (10 g) sugar
Pinch of salt

Preheat the oven to 275°F (130°C).

Slice the figs through crosswise three-quarters of the way above the base.

Place the bay leaves with a pinch of sugar under the top (the stem end) of the figs.

Close and hold in place with a toothpick.

Arrange the figs in a serving dish and sprinkle with the rest of the sugar.

Bake for 15 minutes.

Meanwhile, reduce the peach juice with the bay leaves, sugar, and salt.

When the liquid has reduced by two-thirds, strain it.

Serve the baked figs sprinkled with the reduced peach juice.

The Mediterranean

THE MEDITERRANEAN, GLIMPSED THROUGH SHADY FORESTS
OF CYPRESS AND UMBRELLA PINE, SPEAKS OF AN INIMITABLE,
SUNNY LIFESTYLE. THE RIVIERA SPIRIT IS THAT OF *LA DOLCE VITA*
AND ITS CHARM NEVER WANES.

THAT RIVIERA FEEL

We move on to another property, another challenge, a different story. The final chapter to date in the Compagnie des Hôtels de Montagne saga concerns the Villa Marie in Ramatuelle. Isn't a *bastide* the Provence equivalent of an Italian villa? And anyway, having been in the mountains and the country, it seems natural to head for the sea. The surprise effect is splendidly carried off, and Villa Marie deserves the plaudits. One has to leave the bustling Route des Plages, which leads to the road to Pampelonne, and take a lane whose disconcerting anonymity is startling in such a crowded resort. After another moment's hesitation, the villa appears in the shade of some great trees. Even within the gates, doubts linger, but, as soon as one passes through the little door, the magic begins to weave its spell. A brief saunter down the avenue, and already the gardens offer solace to the eye.

When, a few years ago now, between St Tropez and Ramatuelle, the Sibuets stumbled across a small hotel that was showing its age and beginning to fade away, it was love at first sight. The building itself was nothing special, but it enjoyed the luxury of being protected amid two hectares of pine forest. It was a pocket-sized Eden, sheltered from the noise and the lunacy that is St Tropez. For Jean-Louis, "the site was there. Though the spaces were impressive, the plot had been exploited in a manner we would reject today. The orientations, for example, were all wrong." When the hotel was built, the prevailing aesthetic and concern for quality of life were a far cry from what we demand today. For example, the sea was hardly visible from the hotel, while the parking lot possessed a most splendid view over the bay!

The questions raised by each new building site are soon answered. These range from, why do we like this place, why are we filled with enthusiasm, and how do we best emphasize what we have, to what spaces and what surfaces should we stress? And so on. Then there was the question of making it cost-effective.

Since every space has its key element, the decision was rapidly taken to build the project round the garden, instead of vice versa. Here, more than elsewhere, vegetation predominates. That bond with bountiful nature fosters an atmosphere ideally suited to the location, and always with the quest for a discreet, sophisticated, unpretentious luxury, incorporating the values the Sibuets hold most dear (the family, nature), and which their guests share. Jocelyne decided "to recreate the atmosphere that reigned at one time on the Côte d'Azur," and that she can still recall. Something to do

Enjoy the view over the pine wood, the garden, the countryside, the bay, and the Mediterranean horizon as far as the eye can see. From wherever one stands and looks, the terraces offer a superb vista over a natural spectacle; it all seems a far cry from the hurly-burly of the nearby villages.

with messing about in boats, picnics, pebbles.... A place where high society met for the winter. The realm of the "beautiful people," bursting with a joie de vivre, a carefree cheerfulness. A *dolce vita* that today is talked of in nostalgic tones. A Riviera, updated and reconfigured, whose codes one revisits in this "Italian villa" spirit. She wanted to get back to a Mediterranean style that is no more Italian than Spanish or Moroccan. A style of grandeur that's a little excessive; after all, St Tropez is not far away!

In six months, the surface area of the hotel was doubled and new buildings—restaurant, bar, lobby—were erected in front of the old. They were along the same lines, but with more character, and left room for covered terraces and pergolas. Independent from each other, they left the view uninterrupted and fitted in with the preexisting range of buildings that was itself spruced up with a lick of paint. The thick walls were treated to a coat of plaster or whitewash, the color of the paint chosen being stony or earthy, running from yellow through bister to yellow ocher. The rooms were all rearranged, though the original architecture and local traditions were respected. In optimizing the location, a vast range of parameters was taken into account, from the east-facing exposure to the pernicious effects of the salty air.

"We stuck by the rough terrain, using it in the most natural way we could." Thus, the interior courtyards are havens of peace that serve to keep out the wind, whereas, when it came to planting trees, the property's proximity to the sea was not forgotten, and preference was accorded to those traditional Provence species best adapted to the climate and location. The whole was organized along very Latin lines, with thematic gardens providing a bridge between the various components. "The 'villa' spirit is very close to my sensibility. I wanted to create an atmosphere somewhere between Italian villa and turn-of-the-century beach house, a cross between two highly contemporary influences."

And then, in their search for pastures new, in their desire to rekindle their love of color, to absorb other harmonies, the Sibuets made repeated trips to Italy. As well they might, en route they combed the junk shops, gathering a great bookcase here, and headboards in Florence that immediately found their way back to the Villa Marie. "One returns from traveling, the brain crammed full of images. We see things, record them, and then we forget what it was we liked—but it resurfaces unbeknownst to us, adapted, incorporated, reworked. One can't speak of creation—it's reinterpretation."

Before building work is underway, Jocelyne spends a few days on site to let her eyes get used to the location. Then, the spadework begins. She searches for interconnections, piling up images, portraits, pictures, photographs to achieve that 1950s St Tropez mood, but she feels it's not quite right. Things will only come together after reading a biography of F. Scott Fitzgerald, when she discovered that the first house the famous American author occupied on the Riviera was called the Villa Marie. This information gave her the impetus she'd lacked. The rest took its cue from a pair of Baroque armchairs, whose kitsch is redolent of collector Peggy Guggenheim in her Côte d'Azur years. These were rounded off with 1950s Riviera objects and furnishings likewise unearthed in the vicinity. "The whole business kicked off with these chairs. There was no initial plan of attack, no preconceived idea at the outset; it was more a

A unique view over the Bay of Pampelonne. Timeless opulence in the shade of the umbrella pine, where you can forget the tumult of beach and city. The exceptional geographical location of the villa means that some bedrooms look over the bay, while others give onto a relaxing view of the pine forest.

reaction to a sudden impulse. The objective was to achieve the simplicity of a 'club' style, fresh and modern, but fed by a wealth of tradition. It's hard to find a balance."

She is well aware, too, of what she needs to borrow from the world outside. No point, for example, in depriving oneself of the characteristic notes of deepest Provence, of patinated gilt furniture and brightly colored printed cloths if they turn out worthwhile. The only certainty, since we're at the seaside, is that the atmosphere should be bracing. The whole project is modern, Baroque, functional, and full of curves, so one feels protected and draped in beautiful colors. The same impressions appear in a painting by an artist friend, the vast picture that now hangs in the reception room. A woman at her window, the pines as a backdrop—and the keynote is given.

Finally, there had to be a change from the earlier *bastide* theme. A modern stripy fabric found in Morocco made the difference. "I cut the fabric into curtains that slide on rails and plaids draped over the foot of the bed to keep you snug on chilly nights. To stumble across fabrics that correspond so marvelously to the location was really lucky." They provide definition for the harmonies in the bedrooms, and their tones are quite different from those commonly found in Provence. The curtains in the main rooms are made of woven Italian straw, and a number of armchairs were refurbished with a motif by Alberto Pinto for Patrick Frey, in keeping with the 1950s Riviera mood.

Fine old stone pillars mark the entrance, which opens onto an avenue lined with cypress and umbrella pine. Basking in its pine forest, the villa has the appeal of an Italian residence. Private space is left open, just a touch, to the outside world. The luxuriant gardens are a treat at any hour from the freshness of the early morning to the soft warmth of the gathering evening.

AN EXTRAORDINARY GARDEN

While the interior was being styled the garden was also taking shape. Jean-Louis pored over memoirs by the great English travelers who came back from China or India at the beginning of the 20th century with exotic plants that they proceeded to try out in the mild climate of the Riviera. For their own pleasure, these amateur botanists created landscape gardens to which their tropical plants, palm trees, type specimens, and ornamental trees soon became acclimatized.

Over the years, these extraordinary gardens have modified the whole Côte d'Azur landscape. The opulent gardens of nearby Italy also leave their mark here. "From enfilades to rows, I took up and reorganized certain themes. I added arbors." The garden with its pools, terraces, and little clearings is treated in the manner of an extra outside room: it forges a chain that encircles the estate. The buildings themselves are buried in nature, standing firmly on the hill, but so well integrated that one soon forgets they are there.

The view opens broadly over a landscape that seems oddly close. Decoration is almost superfluous here, when an imaginative nature has woven her own everlasting backdrop, an immense *tableau vivant*, moving, rustling, generously proportioned. The spaces of the garden amount to a natural complement to the house. From lavender to palms, no expense will be spared to return the stand of pines to its former glory. Three thousand species of conifer and plants were brought in to repopulate the landscape, those from the South of France being given pride of place. The umbrella pines open out in splendor, and the rustic spirit of the trees of Provence finds one of its most beautiful expressions here.

Visitors can explore ten thematic gardens of various sizes, punctuated by basins, rows of trees, multileveled terraces, and fountains. Mature and elegant, the

FOLLOWING PAGES: In the lavender garden, one can relax amid glorious color, cradling a fresh *citron pressé* or a *rosé* made by the family. Turquoise dominates a palette all in tints of blue: transparency and reflections for the carafe; a fuller, purer note for the glasses in opaline turquoise; nuanced for the rough linen bag and cushions in re-embroidered cotton, and for the old hammock hanging between two olive trees.

Bold colors, with strong, bright harmonies—here blood-orange table-settings—were deemed essential for the interior courtyard. Painted wrought iron is deployed generously. Steering clear of the banal, only the vintage, the novel, and the limited series are chosen. A number of armchairs were made in a 1940s Riviera style. Flamboyant nature adds the final touches to the decor: the hydrangeas and the generous wisteria, borne on a weathered stone pillar, offer living proof.

fleshy-leaved plants, the palms, aromatic herbs, citrus, aquatic plants, cypresses, giant pines, and so on … each has its domain in which it is a pleasure to lose oneself. Lemon trees thrive in huge, swelling terracotta pots that seem to greet the newcomer, while the many plants and bouquets brightening up the interior echo those in the garden outside.

On one of the garden terraces, suspended in the shade of a tree, hangs a large birdcage. Bought initially as a pretty adjunct to the decor, it was to have been set up inside the house. A wounded bird decided otherwise. Crash-landing in the garden, he was saved, nursed, and made his nest in the cage. Soon, as good as new, he flew off, but the cage remained where it was. As it had, more by luck than judgment, now regained its true function as a birdcage, no one would today dream of moving it.

CORAL, MOTHER OF PEARL, AND SHELLS

From wherever one is in the property the eye settles on blue and green, on the sky and sea. And because the water's edge is close, and everywhere, so are the starfish, shellfish, and mollusks one shares it with. Dotted about the mantelpiece, crammed on to great vases and urns, stuck in mirror frames in the spirit of surrealist fashion, in pictures, over entire walls. "I adore bouquets of shells, and on vacation one should not be surprised to come across something out of the ordinary," Jocelyne Sibuet insists. She also goes in for graphic arrangements. A mass of objects pose for a still-life photograph—a marble table laden with flowers or omnipresent shells. Click!, and freeze-frame.

A persistent feature of the Sibuet's locations is the freedom of movement they allow: the welcoming nooks and crannies where, incognito, you can take the weight off your feet, where light can be controlled. The large drawing room is bathed in a luminous orange. Everything is given dramatic emphasis; the Baroque permeates everything. Old Italian console tables stand cheek by jowl with a venerable Florentine bookcase and the barley-sugar shafts of Venetian lamps. The Baroque bench, a central element, sallies forth in coral red, while the cotton-satin cushions, not to be outdone, boast a pattern in the same color. Next to them, the armchairs try out daring contrasts in tone: black chair, orange cushion. And the modern striped fabrics mix the pot with shades of black on coarse, printed linens.

Throughout the room are soft, yielding sofas that one can happily flop down in, and garden chairs discreetly converted. This is a contemporary treatment for a living room that nonetheless does not forgo old-world comfort. Cheekily, a tiny designer lamp, perfectly color coordinated, does its modest thing on a gueridon. Idiosyncratic harmonies, loud color mixtures, and original materials are, more than ever, the watchwords here. Subtle hues like beige and pale blue join forces with bolder, brighter colors such as turquoise and orange. With ever-so-many precautions, however, since if bright orange suits the sun at the seaside admirably, a strong blue is

In the entrance, the table signed Hervé Thibault recalls the Riviera feel of the dawn of the twentieth century. The patinated Baroque console sports an authentic stoup framed by stone candleholders. In a corner of the drawingroom, on the Italian console, stand two Medici vases, shells, flowers, and some resolutely kitsch candlesticks. Here is the place to be daring. Coral, sharp pinks, turquoise, chocolate…. Bright, striking colors, canvas and satins, and an abundant miscellany of shells for the main drawing room. In the center of the room stands the long black settee with its orange and brown cushions. Light-hearted eclecticism reigns, with Baroque and 1950s styles leading the way.

Here and there, coral and shells of various sizes remind us that the beach is not far away. Gossamer linen lends itself well to idleness. Showered by wisteria, the outside terrace is bedecked with local iron chairs and side tables. The objects standing on the chests of drawers, consoles, or serving tables, are arranged with nothing left to chance. The mistress of the house composes them like so many still lifes. Thus, on an old service table, which was also unearthed locally, the dish and engraving conspire to leave a path for the ivy. The mirror, ornamented with shellwork, reflects the vast drawing room. Meanwhile, the Baroque armchairs revel in their bright colors.

 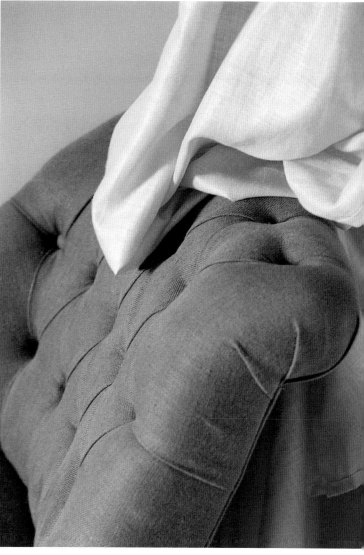

undoubtedly more difficult to handle. Misused, it can quickly pall. However, these warm, dazzling colors unleash every last nuance when the foil is an ubiquitous white, the ideal background against which to set the furniture and the antiques, allowing for some sophisticated variations if one plays with its various shades. Here, the plainness of the limewashed walls is occasionally interrupted by a more colorful note.

Wherever one looks outside, one is struck by the wealth of color. "Originally I started off with transparent whites and beiges, and then orange, coral, and tangerine came into their own in the large sitting room, and turquoise percolated through, a reminder of the great blue yonder. A mutually stimulating dialogue between colors and elements. In fact, there are always connections; I just add the finishing touch." And of course she could not rest before finding the bright orange crockery and the great plates

The gilt wood of the Florentine headboard emerges against the broken harmonies of dominant chestnut and pale blue. The Medici-style stone vase has changed jobs, and now displays its coral like a work of art, a sculpture, on the two-color chest. Linen resurfaces in the upholstery for the easy chairs.

The armchair, discovered in a local antique shop, has been left in its original 1950s condition. The transparency of the linen gauze makes for a subtle intimacy between bathroom

and bedroom. While the headboard has been restored to its former state, in the bathroom the basins in Lens or Cassis stone and the taps and fixtures are state-of-the-art.

of a deep blue for the garden tables. When black is too strong, she replaces it with chocolate as a counter to the gilded wood and aniseed. As for crushed mauve, it is graphically mixed with black. She comes down from Megève to supervise the various stages of the painting, even if it means to having to begin over—as has happened. "The fashionable style stems from very little." Fresher hues are reserved for the restrooms and evoke the grasses growing in disheveled tufts in the countryside, the dark green of thyme, the gray blue of lavender. A quiet range of mauves, yellows, aniseed, and flax appears in the corridors and alcoves. The Italian gilt-wood furniture is associated with Baroque elements, quirky 1950s seats in wrought iron bought in junk shops. The unpretentious furniture is perfect when leant against ancient, grainy walls, where the paint cracks, as if that had always been its place.

The curtains for the bedrooms were made out of a stripy handmade Moroccan fabric that comes in several colors—here it ranges over mauve, pink, and aniseed. The large cushions have been reembroidered by hand. The room combines styles, but the priority is comfort and ease. According to the season, berries or roses gathered from the garden afford extra pleasure to the eye.

DOWN BY
THE WATERFRONT

Large openings, bay windows, covered terraces, pergolas, verandas: Villa Marie lives with its (glass) doors thrown open. The staircases are designed as vast curved sweeps, and it is wonderful to stand for a moment and let the eye wander. The arcades, wrought iron scrolls, Roman tiles, and spicy colors are all subtly blended. Everywhere one finds places where one can rest in the greatest comfort and enjoy the splendid views—be they over one of the inner gardens, towards a fountain, or quite simply a panorama over the sea, of which one can never tire. Slowly but surely the out-of-the-way terrace—top corner for breakfast, bottom corner for the afternoon sun, for idle moments or for a siesta—has become the place to be. It is impossible to resist the temptation to drink in the first or last rays of sunshine, listening to the babbling waters pouring forth from a small fountain, watching the light—diffuse, bright, silky—dance. It is a light that can do and undo anything. Or you can listen out for the cicadas and crickets, or watch the spiraling flight of the cabbage white. As if to temper the glare of the blanching sun, everywhere terracotta tones jostle and vie with tints of red ocher and yellow beige. On one patio, pillars brought from Italy embrace the clambering wisteria, structuring the space. One can only guess at how a curtain would fly around in the wind, were it not tied back with a knot. It retains the heat but lets the light through.

Elsewhere stand Italian terracotta urns and pots planted with cacti, and superbly made large glazed earthenware jars. The local craftsmen and producers were all asked not to depart from the pervading tone. The swimming pool has kept its kidney-bean lines, but the stone walls extending over the rocks give it a mineral feel. It too clings to nature, and it is a joy to lounge around in the shade of the gigantic pines.

Far from the bustle of the port, the peace and quiet of the creeks is within easy reach aboard one of the local boats: *barcasse* or *pointu*. Bayadère cloth remains a great favorite on which to enjoy picnics featuring local delicacies by the water's edge. A picnic on the waterfront is not complete without the flavor of lemon olive oil. Striped deck chairs and cushions create a colorful setting (left). With picnic baskets fulled to bursting, take a stroll alongside the famous port of Saint-Tropez and then settle down for a gourmet feast in a little creek, hidden away from the world (facing page).

Aperitifs

Cocktails

• CUCUMBER AND CELERY JUICE
TO MAKE 1 CUP (250 ML)
INGREDIENTS: 1 small cucumber or $\frac{1}{2}$ large one - 1 stick of celery

Carefully wash the cucumber and celery. Do not peel the cucumber. Cut the cucumber in half and remove the seeds. Place the cucumber and the celery in a blender and blend until smooth. Season to taste and serve very cold.

• APRICOT JUICE WITH LAVENDER
TO MAKE 1 CUP (250 ML)
INGREDIENTS: 5 apricots - 3 tsp lavender essence - 1 sprig of lavender for decoration

Pit the apricots. Put them in a blender with the lavender essence. Serve ice cold with the sprig of lavender as decoration.

• STRAWBERRY AND RASPBERRY JUICE WITH SAGE
TO MAKE 1 CUP (250 ML)
INGREDIENTS: 10 strawberries - 20 raspberries - 3 fresh sage leaves

Carefully wash the strawberries and raspberries and place them in a bowl with the sage leaves. Serve chilled.

Olive Bread

SERVES 10
INGREDIENTS: $\frac{2}{3}$ cup (150 ml) sunflower oil - 6 large eggs - $\frac{2}{3}$ cup (150 ml) whole milk - Salt and pepper - 2 cups (250 g) all-purpose flour - 2 tsp (12 g) baking powder - 1 scant cup (200 g) pitted black olives

Preheat the oven to 350°F (180°C).
Combine the oil, eggs, milk, salt, and pepper. Sift the flour and baking powder into a bowl and combine with the liquid ingredients. Knead the dough until smooth, then incorporate the whole olives.
Line a loaf pan with nonstick baking paper and fill it two-thirds full. Bake for around 45 minutes or until done.

Picnic Menu on the Rocks

Swordfish and Jumbo Shrimp Kabobs

SERVES 4
INGREDIENTS: 1 swordfish fillet, around $10\frac{1}{2}$ oz (300 g) - 8 peeled jumbo shrimps - 1 lemon - 1 lime - 10 fresh sage leaves - Olive oil - 8 wooden skewers

Cut the swordfish fillet into eight cubes.
Split the shrimp in half lengthwise. Cut the lemons and limes into quarters. Arrange a cube of swordfish on a skewer plus 1 quarter of lime, 1 halved shrimp, 1 sage leaf, and 1 quarter of lemon. Repeat the operation for the rest of the skewers. Brush the skewers with oil and broil them or grill on a barbecue.
Just before serving, sprinkle with a little olive oil and the two remaining sage leaves, chopped.

Citrus Salad with Mint

SERVES 4
INGREDIENTS: 2 grapefruits - 4 oranges - 1 lemon - 1 cup (250 ml) water - $\frac{1}{3}$ cup (100 g) sugar - 2 mint sprigs - 2 tsp orange-flower water

This recipe should be prepared on the day before it is to be served.
Peel the grapefruits, oranges, and the lemon. Cut out the white parts and reserve the rind for decoration.
Separate the segments of grapefruit, orange, and lemon. Bring the water and sugar to the boil, then leave this syrup to cool.
Combine the citrus segments with the syrup, fresh mint leaves and orange-flower water. Leave to macerate overnight. Serve chilled.

PICNIC MENU ON THE ROCKS

COOKED VEGETABLE SALAD

SERVES 4
INGREDIENTS: 2 zucchini - 1 eggplant - Olive oil - 1 red bell pepper - 6 tomatoes - 9 fl oz (250 ml) olive oil - Salt and pepper - 1 garlic clove, softened by baking and crushed - Juice of 1 lemon - A few black olives - 4 tsp (20 g) parmesan

Slice the zucchini and eggplant into thin strips and broil them in a dry frying pan. Then leave them to marinate in 4 tablespoons of the olive oil. Grind a little pepper over them.
Bake the bell peppers in the oven at 300°F (150°C) for 15 minutes. Skin them, cut them open, and discard the seeds and ribs. Slice into thin strips. Add them to the zucchini and eggplant marinade.
Quarter the tomatoes without cutting right through and scoop out the pulp.
Dry the tomato "petals" in a cool oven at 110 °C (225°F) for 1 hour.
Drain the eggplant, zucchini, and peppers.
Mix them with the tomato petals. Season with a little olive oil, the crushed garlic clove, lemon juice, olives, and parmesan.

PIZZETTA WITH TOMATOES AND OLIVES

SERVES 4
INGREDIENTS: 4 x 1³/₄ oz (50 g) puff dough - 4 tbs tapenade - 4 vines of cherry tomatoes (about 24 tomatoes) - 15 pitted black olives

Preheat the oven to 180°C (350°F).
Roll out the puff dough into 4 rectangles.
Spread the tapenade over the dough, then arrange the tomatoes and whole olives on top.
Bake for 30 minutes.

NIÇOISE FRIED SLICES

SERVES 4
INGREDIENTS: 2 scant cups (200 g) green beans - 2 large waxy potatoes, diced - 2 eggs - 1/2 long cucumber or 1 small cucumber - 1 small red bell pepper - 2 tomatoes - 1 tbs olive oil - 4 slices wholewheat bread - 7 oz (200 g) tapenade - 8 anchovy fillets, soaked in milk to remove salt

Boil the beans and potatoes separately.
Hard boil the eggs.
Peel the cucumber and skin the pepper.
Cut the tomatoes into quarters. Heat the olive oil in a frying pan and cook the slices of bread on both sides until colored. Spread them with the tapenade, arrange the other ingredients on top, and serve.

MELON SOUP

SERVES 4
INGREDIENTS: 2 medium melons - 2¹/₂ tbs (50 g) sugar - 1 cup (250 ml) sparkling wine - 3 sprigs of mint

Peel and de-seed the melons. Combine their flesh with the sugar and sparkling wine, and strain through a conical sieve.
Serve very cold with fresh mint.

LUNCH ON THE TERRACE

LOBSTER AND ASPARAGUS SALAD

SERVES 4
INGREDIENTS: 1 vanilla pod - 5 tbs olive oil -
12 asparagus spears - 2 lobsters, approx. 1 lb 2oz (500 g) each -
1 lemon - 12 capers - 5 sprigs fresh basil

The night before, split the vanilla pod in two
lengthwise and let it macerate all night in the
olive oil.
On the day, trim the asparagus stalks to remove
the woody part and cook the tips in salted
boiling water for 10 minutes.
Plunge the lobsters into boiling water and
cook them for 15 minutes once the water has
come back to the boil. Rinse under cold
running water and shell them.
Make a dressing by combining the lemon
juice, capers, and vanilla-flavored olive oil,
beating lightly.
Arrange the asparagus with pieces of lobster
on a serving platter, sprinkle with the dressing,
and serve.

SQUID INK RISOTTO

SERVES 4
INGREDIENTS: 12–16 small squid (calamari) - 2 shallots,
chopped - 1 tbs olive oil - 1 lb 2 oz (500 g) risotto (short-grained)
rice - About 2 cups (500 ml) chicken or veal stock - Coarse salt -
Grated parmesan - 1 tbs Tio Pepe sherry - $3^1/_2$ tbs (50g) butter -
Ink from the squid

Clean and prepare the small squid, allowing
3–4 per person. Sauté the chopped shallots in
the olive oil, add the rice and add enough stock
to cover, season with coarse salt. Simmer
for 12 minutes on a low heat, then add a small
handful of parmesan, the sherry, the butter, and
a small ladleful (about $1/_2$ cup) of stock to make
the rice creamy. Continue cooking the risotto.
Finally add a tablespoon of squid ink.
While the risotto is cooking, sauté the
squid over a high heat for 7 minutes. Remove
from the heat and season to taste.
Serve the risotto in soup plates, arranging the
squid on top. Finish with a little olive oil and
a pinch of sea salt.

LUNCH ON THE TERRACE

BAKED GILTHEAD BREAM OR SEA BREAM

SERVES 2
INGREDIENTS:
1 gilthead bream or sea bream weighing about 1 lb 2 oz–1 lb 5 oz (500–600 g), de-scaled and gutted - Salt and pepper - Olive oil - Thyme - Bay leaf - 1–2 star anise - Rosemary - Dried fennel - Preserved tomatoes, sliced

Wash and trim the fish. Preheat the oven to 350°F (180°C).

Season the fish with salt and pepper and brush it with olive oil. Sprinkle with the herbs, including the dried fennel.

In an ovenproof dish, arrange rounds of preserved tomatoes and sprinkle with a little olive oil. Place the bream on top. Sprinkle with more olive oil and bake for 10–12 minutes.

LEMON MOUSSE

MAKES 8 GLASSES
INGREDIENTS:

LEMON CREAM:
3 whole eggs - 2 egg yolks - $^2/_3$ cup (150 g) sugar - 3 lemons, juice squeezed

Combine the sugar, whole eggs, and yolks. Add the lemon juice and a little butter. Cook, stirring constantly, until the mixture thickens, then allow to cool. Refrigerate until required.

LIMONCELLO JELLO:
Limoncello is an Italian lemon liqueur made from lemons, sugar, and clear spirits such as vodka.
1 tbs unflavored gelatin - 3 cups (750 ml) water - 1$^3/_4$ cups (400 g) honey - 1 scant cup (200 ml) Limoncello

Soften the gelatin in two tablespoons of cold water. Heat the water, honey, and Limoncello to just below the boil. Remove from the heat and add the softened gelatin. Cool, then refrigerate.

LIGHT LEMON CREAM:
2 cups (500 ml) whipping cream - 1 cup (250 ml) lemon cream (see above)

Whip the cream until stiff, then combine it with the lemon cream and refrigerate until required.

TO ASSEMBLE THE MOUSSE:
In a large glass bowl, start with a layer of the rest of the lemon cream, then a layer of the light lemon cream, and finally a layer of the limoncello jello, keeping the layers separate. Refrigerate for at least 3 hours before serving.

USEFUL ADDRESSES

To call France from abroad dial 0033 and omit the first 0 of the local number.

THE ALPS

FOIRE DE LA SAINT OURS
Piazza Chanaux - 11000 Aoste
01 65 23 66 27
Carved wood articles. A very fine
display of mountain crafts.
January 30 and 31 and the week
before August 15.

Philippe Bottolier Depois
74360 Vacheresse
04 50 73 10 27
Wooden sculpture, molds, salt
cellars, and more.

ANTIQUES

CATHERINE NAVARRO
Ferme du Cruet
Route de Praz Sur Arly
74120 Megève - 04 50 58 98 38
Decorative objects and quality
folk-art furniture.

VEYRET ANTIQUAIRES
Route d'Annecy
74230 Thônes - 04 50 02 15 56
Exceptional folk-art furniture
(some remarkable pieces
available).

INTERIOR DECORATION

DOGUE BLEU
168 avenue Michel Croz
74400 Chamonix
04 50 53 34 01
For wooden hearts carved by
local guides.

GALERIE SAINT BENOÎT
4 rue Guillaume Fichet
73000 Chambéry
04 79 70 04 45
For pictures and prints on
mountain themes.

POIL DE CAROTTE
34 route de Saint François
de Sale - 74120 Megève
04 50 21 12 81
For lamps and exterior lighting
and decorative objects.

LE COMPTOIR DE MEGÈVE
112 rue de Saint François
de Salles - 74120 Megève
04 50 58 72 94
Furniture and decorative objects
from the mountains with a
pronounced Austrian flavor;
hunting trophies.

FABRICS

FILATURE ARPIN FRÈRES
La Fabrique - 73700 Seez
04 79 07 28 79
Woolen cloth used to make
Alpine hunting breeches.
For pretty blankets, embroidered
plaids and woolen throws in a
wide range of colors.

TAPESTRY

SEINERA DÉCORATION
18 avenue Paul Girod
73400 Ugine - 04 79 37 35 22

POTTERY

FABRIQUE POTERIE
SAVOYARDE
Chemin de la Poterie
74570 Evires - 04 50 62 01 90
Very fine wedding dishes and
exceptional earthenware pieces.
An attractive private museum
belonging to the Herman family.

POTERIE DE MARNAZ
74460 Marnaz - 04 50 98 35 49
Traditional Savoyard pottery,
founded 1895. One of the oldest
in the region, active for several
generations.

POTERIE ARTISANALE
Route nationale 203
74800 Etaux
Traditional pottery.

BOOKS

LIBRAIRIE DES ALPES
1 rue Casimir Périer
38000 Grenoble - 04 76 51 57 98
All sorts of books on the
mountains.

GOURMET ADDRESSES

DANIEL BOUJON
7 rue Saint Sébastien
74200 Thonon les Bains
04 50 71 07 68
Savoyard cheeses distributed
throughout the rest of France.

GLAÇONS DE MEGÈVE
Quai du Prieuré - 74120 Megève
04 50 21 02 12
Chocolate and praline specialties
unique to Megève.

BOUTIQUE AU CHOCOLAT
176 rue Charles Feige
74120 Megève - 04 50 21 01 64
Quality chocolate maker with a
number of specialties, such as
chardons.

LES JARDINS DU COTEAUX
DE PASSY
Josiane Chappaz
74190 Passy - 04 50 78 30 80
Vegetables and plants grown
according to the best traditions.
Every Friday morning at Megève
market.

PLANTS

GRUSKA
76 chemin Foray
73160 Cognin - 04 79 68 75 51
For Alpine garden and mountain
plants.

PORK BUTCHERS

MAISON PINEAU
30 route de Flaine
74300 Magland - 04 50 34 71 13
For its celebrated charcuterie and
Magland *saucisses*.

OTHER FAVORITE SPOTS

LE REFUGE DU MIAGE
1276 route des Contamines
74170 Saint Gervais les Bains
04 50 93 22 91
Mountain refuge at the foot of the
Miage glacier. Renowned for its
omelets and charcuterie.

DOMINIQUE MUFFAT
Domaine de la Sasse
Le Planey - 74120 Megève
06 09 90 30 29
Bison farm with *table d'hôtes*
restaurant.

RESTAURANT DU
MONTENVERS
Site du Montenvert Mer de Glace
74400 Chamonix Mont Blanc
04 50 53 87 70
At the foot of the Mer de Glace,
an atmosphere early 20th-century
Alpinists would recognize!

THE SOUTH

PLANTS

MICHEL SEMINI
Rue Saint Frusquin
84220 Gault - 04 90 72 38 50
For gardens in southern climes.

JEAN-CLAUDE APPY
Route de Jaucas
Saint Andrieu - 81220 Rousillon
04 90 05 62 94
Excellent choice of plants from
the smallest to the most lofty,
including centuries-old olive trees.

LE JARDIN DES LAVANDES
La Ferme aux Lavandes
Route du Mont Ventoux
84390 Sault - 04 90 64 14 97
A lavender farm featuring a
number of medicinal varieties.

ANTIQUES

LEMOINE ANTIQUITÉS
Le Carré d'Herbes
84800 L'Isle sur Sorgue

ANTIQUAIRE F. DERVIEUX
5 rue Vermon - 13200 Arles
04 90 96 02 39
Very fine Provençal furniture.

NICOD GÉRARD
115 chemin Chapelle
84800 L'Isle sur la Sorgue
04 90 38 20 38

Furniture and unusual objects left as nature intended.

OBJET DE HASARDS
13 avenue Quatres Otages
84800 L'Isle sur la Sorgue
04 90 38 54 58
Splendid furniture and old articles. Some original and unexpected pieces.

DECORATION

SACHA DÉCORATION
Place Albert Roure
84560 Ménerbes - 04 90 72 41 28
Good selection of crockery and excellent household linen.

LE GRAND MAGASIN
24 rue de la Commune
13210 Saint Remy de Provence
04 90 92 18 79
Art gallery, interior decoration, and everyday articles.

GALERIES TROPÉZIENNES
56 rue Gambetta
83990 Saint Tropez
04 94 97 02 21
For crockery, very pretty table settings, and tablecloths. Diverse everyday items (lanterns, hammocks, etc.).

MAISON DES LICES
2 boulevard Louis Blanc
83990 Saint Tropez
04 94 97 64 64
For crockery and decorative objects.

MANUFACTURE DES TAPIS
DE COGOLIN
6 boulevard Louis Blanc
83310 Cogolin - 04 94 55 70 65
Hand-woven tufted carpets made-to-order.

NONO GIRARD
La Capucine
86 allée Jean Jaures
84200 Carpentras - 04 90 60 36 58
Very fine garden furniture from the Comtat Vénaissin—perfect for creating that seductive Southern décor.

ATELIER DE PEINTURE
Hervé Thibault - Le Village
84220 Les Beaumettes
04 90 72 28 78
Especially noteworthy for superb frescoes and atmospheric backdrops that can be sampled in the Hôtel Cour des Loges, in Lyon.

CONSERVATOIRE DES OCRES
ET PIGMENTS APPLIQUÉS
Ancienne usine Mathieu D 104
84220 Roussillon - 04 90 05 66 69
For paints and coating treatments.

MATERIALS

JEAN CHABAUD
ZI route de Gargas
84400 Apt - 04 90 74 07 61
Antiques and old building materials. Weathered stone.

PROVENCE RETROUVÉE
2761 route d'Apt
84800 L'Isle sur la Sorgue
04 90 38 52 62
Fine building materials. Excellent choice of character pieces.

VERNIN CARREAUX D'APT
Quai St Eyriès - 84480 Bonnieux
04 90 04 63 04
Enamel tiling with a splendid range of hand-applied colors.

POTTERY

POTERIE RAVEL
Avenue des Goums
13400 Aubagne
04 42 82 42 00
For traditional earthenware pots for outside.

L'ATELIER LOUIS SICCARD
2 boulevard Emile Combes
13400 Aubagne
04 42 70 12 92
Traditional Provence-style pottery. Wonderful traditional Provençal cigales (ornamental cicada models) and pretty local yellow crockery.

FAUCON FAÏENCE D'APT
286 avenue de la Libération
84400 Apt - 04 90 74 15 31
Various local ceramics and pottery.

ANTONI PITOT
Ponty Nord - 84 220 Gault
04 90 72 22 79
Pottery with some extremely original pieces. Certain models can be made-to-order.

POTERIE DE HAUTE PROVENCE
Route de Nyons
26220 Dieulefit
04 75 46 42 10
In a traditional potters' village in the Drôme, a fine selection of crockery and dishes.

FABRICS

LA MAISON BIEHN
7 avenue des Quatre Otages
84800 L'Isle sur la Sorgue
04 90 20 89 04
Old-style Provençal printed plain-weave cloths.
Historic *boutis* and old weaves. All the charm of Provence.

BRUN DE VIAN TIRAN
2 cours Victor Hugo
84800 L'Isle sur la Sorgue
04 90 38 00 81
Plaids and coverlets in Arles merinos.

EDITH MEZARD
Château de L'Ange
84220 Lumières
04 90 72 36 41
Linen, hand-embroidered household cloth. Beautifully displayed in outhouses belonging to the Château de l'Ange.

LA BOUTIQUE DE FRANCINE
1 avenue Julien Guigue
84800 L'Isle sur la Sorgue
04 90 38 55 81
Very beautiful collection of *boutis* and old textiles. Specialists in fine historic weaves.

MARIA
4 avenue Julien Guigue
Marché du quai de la Gare
84800 Avignon - 04 90 38 58 02
For old linen and large embroidered lavender bags.

ATELIER DU PRESBYTÈRE
10 rue du Presbytère - 30300
Vallabregues - 04 66 59 37 37
Old linen, very fine cloth laundry bags and household textiles.

GOURMET ADDRESSES

CAFÉ DE FRANCE
67 place Bouquerie
84400 Apt - 04 90 74 22 01
In season, the best scrambled eggs with truffles in the region for Saturday lunch; market days at Apt.

LE CARRÉ D'HERBES
13 avenue des Quatre Otages
84800 l'Isle sur Sorgue
04 90 38 62 95
In the heart of the Carré at l'Isle sur Sorgue, an unpretentious lunch amidst a host of antiques.

LE FOURNIL
5 place Carnot - 84480 Bonnieux
04 90 75 83 62
Cuisine with a Southern accent.

MAISON DE LA TRUFFE
ET DU VIN
Place de l'horloge
84560 Ménerbes - 04 90 72 52 10
Wine tastings and beginners' courses on wine science.

LE MARCHÉ DE COUSTELLET
84660 Maubec / Coustellet
Typical Provençal market (vegetables, fruits, flowers…).
Every Sunday morning and Wednesdays from 6 p.m.
High quality and small producers.

LES DÉLICES DU LUBÉRON
Avenue du 8 Mai
84800 Isle sur Sorgue
04 90 20 77 37
Maker of Provençal specialties including *tapenade*, great for accompanying an aperitif.

CONFISEUR LILIAMAND
5 avenue Albert Schweitzer
13210 Saint-Remy-de-Provence
04 90 92 11 08
Confectionery.

DOMAINE D'ESTOUBLON
Chemin Auge - 13990 Font Vieille
04 90 54 64 00
Fine olive-oil barrel house
supplied by various estates.

BOOKS

LIBRAIRIE DUMAS
16 rue des Marchands
84400 Apt - 04 90 74 23 81
One of the finest bookshops in
the region with a wide choice on
Provence.

LE KAYAK VERT
La Beaume - 84800 La Fontaine
de Vaucluse - 04 90 20 35 44
For a summer descent of the
River Sorgue or to listen to
stories by Michel Melani.

VARIOUS

LUBÉRON INVESTISSEMENT
Quartier la Combe
84220 Gordes - 04 90 72 07 55
Vincent Bœuf will help you
unearth the house of your
dreams in the Lubéron.

A FEW OTHER PLACES WORTH DISCOVERING

ATELIER PAUL CÉZANNE
9 avenue Paul Cézanne
13100 Aix en Provence
On the Collines d'Aix.

MUSÉE ARLATEN
29 rue de la République
13200 Arles - 04 90 93 58 11
A good collection of paintings.
Fine illustrations in the Provençal
tradition.

SOULEIADO
Musée Charles DEMERY
39 rue Proudhon - 13150
Tarascon - 04 90 91 50 11
Excellent collection of block-
printed fabrics.

MUSÉE DU TIRE-BOUCHON
Le Chataignier - Route de
Cavaillon - 84560 Ménerbes
04 90 72 41 58
Very extensive collection of
corkscrews assembled by
the mayor of Ménerbes,
Yves Rousset-Rourard.

CHÂTEAU DE LOURMARIN
Impasse du Pont du Temple
84160 Lourmarin
04 90 68 15 23
Outdoor summer concerts.

MY FAVORITE PRODUCERS

Fabrics

DESIGNERS GUILD
10 rue Saint Nicolas
75012 Paris - 01 44 67 80 70

PIERRE FREY
2 rue Furstenberg - 75006 Paris
01 46 33 73 00

THORP OF LONDON
10 avenue Villars - 75007 Paris
01 47 53 76 37

LE IMPRESSIONS EDITION
Dominique Kieffer
8 rue Herold - 75001 Paris
01 42 21 32 44

DÉCORTEX
7 rue de Furstenberg
75006 Paris - 01 40 51 01 22

Interior decoration

EMERY ET COMPAGNIE
18 passage Main d'Or
75011 Paris - 01 44 87 02 02
Fine choice of paints with a soft
palette, cement, tiling, and
some cloths.
Craft decoration materials.
Wrought-iron furniture.

MISE EN DEMEURE
27 rue du Cherche Midi
75006 Paris - 01 45 48 83 79
Collection of furniture,
objects, copies and a
superb selection of large
chandeliers.

THE COMPLETE LIST OF PROPERTIES OWNED BY HÔTELS DE MONTAGNE

MEGÈVE

Les Fermes de Marie **
Chemin de Riante Colline
74120 Megève
Tel.: 04 50 93 03 10
Fax: 04 50 93 09 84
www.fermesdemarie.com
contact@fermesdemarie.com

Le Mont-Blanc **
Place de L'Eglise
74120 Megève
Tel.: 04 50 21 20 02
Fax: 04 50 21 45 28
www.hotelmontblanc.com
contact@montblanc.com

Le Lodge Park **
100 rue d'Arly
74120 Megève
Tel.: 04 50 93 05 03
Fax: 04 50 93 09 52
www.lodgepark.com
contact@lodgepark.com

Au Coin du Feu **
Route du Téléphérique de
Rochebrune
74120 Megève
Tel.: 04 50 21 04 94
Fax: 04 50 21 20 15
www.coindufeu.com
contact@coindufeu.com

**The ChaTel. and Hauteluce
properties**
These two stunning chalets on
the Mont d'Arbois plateau, are
available to rent with full hotel
services. For more information
contact Fermes de Marie.

MÉNERBES

La Bastide de Marie **
Route de Bonnieux
Quartier de la Verrerie
84560 Ménerbes
Tel.: 04 90 72 30 20
Fax: 04 90 72 54 20
www.labastidedemarie.com
contact@labastidedemarie.com

Les Propriétés Grenache Syrah
These two exceptional properties
opposite to La Bastide de Marie,
are available to rent with full hotel
services. For more information
contact La Bastide de Marie.

Domaine de Marie
Route de Bonnieux
Quartier de la Verrerie
84 560 Ménerbes
Tel.: 04 90 72 54 23
Fax: 04 90 72 54 24
www.c-h-m.com
dme-de-marie@wanadoo.fr
Found in the heart of the Lubéron
nature reserve, this vineyard
spreads over sixty acres and pro-
duces red, white, and rosé wines.

LYON

Cour des Loges **
2-4-6-8, rue du Bœuf
69005 Lyon
Tel.: 04 72 77 44 44
Fax: 04 72 40 93 61
www.courdesloges.com
contact@courdesloges.com

RAMATUELLE ST-TROPEZ

Villa Marie **
Chemin Val de Rian
83350 Ramatuelle
Tel.: 04 94 97 40 22
Fax: 04 94 97 37 55
www.villamarie.com
contact@villamarie.com

Alpine recipes

CHRISTMAS RECIPES

Chestnut Soup

Sautéed Duck Foie Gras

Roast Turkey with Dried Fruit Compote
 in Honey

Brandied Raspberries

Berry Jello

Christmas Stars

Mont Blanc

LUNCH IN THE ALPINE FOOTHILLS

Cold Nettle and Herb Soup

Open-faced Sandwiches

Crozets with Carrots

Rabbit with Wild Thyme

Berthoud

Blueberry Tart

DINNER IN THE CHALET

Pumpkin, Bacon, and Truffle Soup

Polenta Square

Vanilla Pears in Syrup

Mulled Wine

Shoulder of Veal with Porcini

Risotto

Bugnes (Kindling Cookies)

Pears in Red Wine

DELIGHTS OF THE DAY

Wholegrain Muesli

Christmas Hot Chocolate

Tarentais Cake

Rum Cake

Florentines

Provençal recipes

APERITIFS

Open-faced Baby Vegetable
 Sandwiches

Yellow and Red Tomato Terrine with Basil
 and Goat Milk Yogurt

Toasts with Sheep's Milk Cheese
 and Goat Cheese

LUNCHEON UNDER THE LIME TREE

Bastide Tomato Soup with Olive Oil
 and Chopped Pistachios

Broiled Eggplant

Goat Cheese Marinade

Bastide Herb Tea

Sun-dried Tomatoes on the Vine

Red Plum Tart

HARVEST MENU

Terrine of Dressed Leeks and Chicken
 Liver Mousse

Apple Dumplings

Provençal Beef Stew with Yellow Chanterelles
 and Broiled Waxy Potatoes

DINNER FOR TWO

Provençal Meatballs in Vine Leaves

Warm Vegetable Salad

Baked Figs with Bay Leaves

Mediterranean recipes

APERITIFS

Cucumber and Celery Juice

Apricot Juice with Lavender

Strawberry and Raspberry Juice with Sage

Olive Bread

PICNIC MENU ON THE ROCKS

Swordfish and Jumbo Shrimp Kabobs

Citrus Salad with Mint

Cooked Vegetable Salad

Pizzetta with Tomatoes and Olives

Niçoise Fried Slices

Melon Soup

LUNCH ON THE TERRACE

Lobster and Asparagus Salad

Squid Ink Risotto

Baked Gilthead Bream or Sea Bream

Lemon Mousse

Translated from the French by
David Radzinowicz and Josephine Bacon
Copyediting: Penelope Isaac
Typesetting: Barbara Kekus
Proofreading: Fui Lee Luk
Color Separation: Penez Editions, Lille

Distributed in North America by Rizzoli
International Publications, Inc.

Simultaneously published in French
as *La Maison de nos Vacances*
© Éditions Flammarion, 2005
English-language edition
© Éditions Flammarion, 2005

05 06 07 4 3 2 1

www.editions.flammarion.com

FC0473-05-III
ISBN: 2-0803-0473-9
EAN 9782080304735
Dépôt légal: 03/2005

Printed in Italy by Canale